GOD'S POLITICIAN

God's Politician

William Wilberforce's Struggle

Garth Lean

HELMERS & HOWARD
Colorado Springs

Published by Helmers & Howard, Publishers, Inc.,
P.O. Box 7407, Colorado Springs, CO 80933 USA.

First published in Great Britain by
Darton, Longman & Todd, Ltd.

Library of Congress Cataloging-in-Publication Data

Lean, Garth
    God's Politician.

    Bibliography: p.
    Includes index.
    1. Wilberforce, William, 1759–1833. 2. Great Britain—
Politics and government—1760–1820. 3. Great Britain—
Politics and government—1820–1830. 4. Politicians—
Great Britain—Biography. 5. Abolitionists—Great Britain—
Biography. I. Title.
DA522.W6L43   1987   326'.092'4 [B]   87-23705
ISBN: 0-939443-03-1

Printed in the United States of America

*It is not revolutions and upheavals
That clear the road to new and better days,
But revelations, lavishness and torments
Of someone's soul, inspired and ablaze.*
                                    Boris Pasternak

*Wilberforce proved that one man can change
his times, but he cannot do it alone.*
                                    John Pollock

*God Almighty has set before me two great
objects—the suppression of the slave
trade and the reformation of manners.*
                                    William Wilberforce

To
my wife, Margot,
and to Geoffrey, Judy, and Mary,
gratefully for their comradeship
through the years

By the same author:

Brave Men Choose
John Wesley, Anglican
Good God, It Works!
Rebirth of a Nation?
On the Tail of a Comet:
The Life of Frank Buchman

With Sir Arnold Lunn:
The New Morality
The Cult of Softness
Christian Counter-Attack

With Sydney Cook:
The Black and White Book

Contents

Foreword

IN A DAY WHEN the relationship between religion and politics is
so hotly debated, Garth Lean's book might arouse skepticism:
to many, "God's politician" seems a contradiction in terms.
The life of William Wilberforce shows why it is not. Wilberforce did not confuse or merge the church with the state;
but he did bring transcendent moral values to bear on the
political processes—and thus the society—of his day. Those
who today complain that "you can't legislate morality!" could,
however, only salute Wilberforce's fight to legislate his moral
viewpoint that England's slave trade of the late 18th century
was wrong.

Even the most skeptical cynic about the role of religion in
public life would not denigrate Wilberforce's decades-long
battle against this barbaric evil. And even the most apathetic
Christian must be inspired by Wilberforce's determined obedience to the Christ who called him to oppose injustice.

That is why Garth Lean's book is so important. It is one of
the best of the Wilberforce biographies; *God's Politician* tells
this great saint's story concisely yet completely. Here was a

Christian who put his faith into action in the political arena and persevered for years to outlaw one of the most inhumane—and profitable—practices in the world of his day.

The slave trade generated millions of pounds sterling for the English economy; its tentacles stretched through government to the elegant drawing rooms of the powerful. Wilberforce confronted this tyrant of self-interest; such courage won him insults, opposition, and disgrace. Conversely, he also lived to see his name blessed by thousands of black men and women who could now grant a new legacy of freedom to their descendants.

His battle cost not only the national self-interest, but also his own. Many historians cite Wilberforce as the likely candidate to have succeeded William Pitt as Prime Minister—had he not taken up the unpopular fight against the slave trade.

But for Wilberforce, personal ambition had been surrendered the day he made his dogged decision for Christ—a refreshing testimony in our day when the Christian faith is so often proclaimed as the ultimate enhancement of self-interest, self-esteem, and success. Wilberforce's relationship with God did not enhance his political career; but his obedience to God's standards of justice bore witness to the everlasting Kingdom of God.

Thus this little man with the piercing blue eyes and the upturned nose stands as a giant in the modern history of the faith: God's man, confronting evil in the place where he could fight it best—the battleground of the British Parliament. In this, he was truly God's politician.

Garth Lean's is a book I have reread often. As is the case in all of Garth's writing, he has packed a tremendous amount of information in an eminently readable and memorable style. I am grateful to Helmers & Howard for republishing this fine book in the U.S.; I pray it will stimulate thousands of American Christians to follow Wilberforce's example. His dual passion for both the eradication of injustice and inhumanity, as well as the Christian conversion of his countrymen, served not only the England of his day, but the Kingdom of God of which he was ultimately—and is eternally—a citizen.

CHARLES W. COLSON
WASHINGTON, DC
NOVEMBER, 1987

Author's Note

I FIRST READ IN DEPTH about William Wilberforce in 1957 during convalescence from an illness, and the resulting sketch of his life appeared in my first book *Brave Men Choose* (1960). It was quoted in several Parliaments and inspired a successful West End play, *Mr. Wilberforce, M.P.*, by Alan Thornhill.

At that time little had been written about Wilberforce, apart from his sons' five-volume biography, Sir Reginald Coupland's classic biography of 1923, and Ernest Howse's provocative study of the Clapham brotherhood, *Saints in Politics* (1952). Since then, two monumental biographies, one by Robert Furneaux (1974) and the other by John Pollock (1977) have appeared, as well as shorter studies like that of Oliver Warner (1962). Pollock and Furneaux, in particular, had access to much new material, and I am indebted to them, as well as to the others, both for facts and for quotations.

The object of this little book is to draw out the qualities and methods which made Wilberforce and his friends so uniquely effective in altering the spirit of their age. Consequently it is thematic rather than strictly chronological, and I

have not cluttered the text with references and many foot-
notes.

Sometime after the British edition of *God's Politician* was
published, a nationwide campaign to inform the present
generation of Wilberforce's work was launched by a distinguished committee. I wrote the keynote material which was
sent with an information pack to educational and other local
authorities throughout the country, and also an introduction
which was printed in the Order of Service of Thanksgiving in
Westminster Abbey at which the Speaker of the House of
Commons gave the address and the Prince of Wales laid a
wreath on Wilberforce's tomb.

At the same time, the Church of England allotted July
28th as a Saint's Day in his name, the only politician so
designated for hundreds of years.

Acknowledgement of quotations is given in the text, and
the details of books, publishers, and editions quoted or
consulted are listed in the Select Bibliography. I want
particularly to thank authors and publishers who have given
me permission to quote longer passages, including John
Pollock (Constable and Co. Ltd. and, in paperback, Lion
Publishing); Robin Furneaux, Earl of Birkenhead (Hamish
Hamilton Ltd.) and Ian Bradley (Jonathan Cape, Chatto,
Bodley Head and Cape Services Ltd.), together with Edward
Arnold, Publishers, Ltd. for permission to quote from E. M.
Forster's *Marianne Thornton*; B. T. Batsford Ltd. in respect of
Oliver Warner's *William Wilberforce*; Chatto & Windus
(Chatto, Bodley Head and Cape Services Ltd.) in respect of
Muriel Jaeger's *Before Victoria*; Hodder and Stoughton Ltd.
in respect of J. Wesley Bready's *England before and after
Wesley*, and Hutchinson General Books (Hutchinson Publish-
ing Group) in respect of John Marlowe's *The Puritan Mind in
English Life*.

I would like also to thank Mr. and Mrs. Graham Turner for
much valuable help and advice, and Mrs. Evann Garrison and
Miss Edith-Anne Ramsay for their manifold secretarial skills.
Above all, I am grateful to many friends and colleagues who

have shown me that the seemingly impossible can still become possible today as in Wilberforce's times.

G. D. L.

Introduction:
Britain at the Time of Wilberforce

WILLIAM WILBERFORCE WAS BORN on August 24, 1759, Britain's *annus mirabilis* (wonderful year) in which General James Wolfe captured Quebec, and the French were defeated in crucial land and sea battles. Two years earlier, General Robert Clive had established British predominance in India at the decisive Battle of Plassey, and by 1760 the conquest of French Canada and Spanish Florida were ceded to Britain.

Until 1740 it could be said that Britain possessed a number of separate colonies in the West Indies and North America, mainly for the purposes of trade. Now, suddenly and almost by accident, she was in possession of a worldwide territorial empire. Under the Elder Pitt, now Lord Chatham, she was beginning to look like the coming world power.

As Wilberforce grew to manhood, it became clear how ill-prepared Britain's rulers were for such an eventuality. The mishandling of the American colonists by George III and his uninspired Prime Minister, Lord North, together with the growing maturity of the colonists themselves, resulted in the American Revolution—then regarded in Britain as a disaster, but later to prove a blessing for Britain and the world.

For most of the rest of Wilberforce's active years, Britain, while learning slowly how to care better for her remaining dependencies, was engaged first with the repercussions of the French Revolution and then with the rise and triumphs of Napoleon. The Revolution, with its bloody excesses, frightened many of Britain's rulers into far too repressive attitudes toward unrest at home, a fear which persisted long after the danger had passed. Napoleon's military threat, however, was real enough. Like Hitler more than a century later, he conquered most of Europe and expected to invade England. That threat was not removed until Nelson's victory at the Battle of Trafalgar in 1805, and it was not until 1815 that his military power was broken by the Duke of Wellington at the Battle of Waterloo. It was in the middle of this war, after twenty years of struggle and disappointment, that Wilberforce succeeded in getting a bill for the abolition of the slave trade passed through both Houses of Parliament.

Unlike the United States, Britain has never had a written constitution, but one that grew up through the centuries by custom, usage, Act of Parliament, and judicial decisions. By the eighteenth century it had evolved into the beginnings of a constitutional monarchy. As early as 1729, the great French historian Montesquieu wrote after a visit to England: "England is the freest country in the world. I make no exception of any republic. And I call it free because the sovereign, whose person is controlled and limited, is unable to inflict any imaginable harm on anyone." This observation, as we shall see as Wilberforce's story unrolls, could be an oversimplification, and certainly did not mean that social position lacked its privileges or that those privileges were generally used unjustly. What Montesquieu looked for in a constitution were two elements—that it should be "mixed," combining the distinctive principles of monarchy, aristocracy, and democracy; and that there should be clear distinction between the three departments of government—the legislature, the executive, and the judicature. These elements were, he believed, present in Britain.

For several centuries before Wilberforce was born, England had theoretically been governed by the King and by Parliament. Parliament consisted of two Houses: the Lords, hereditary or created by the sovereign, and the Commons, elected by "the people." In fact, the power of the three elements had varied from time to time, partly due to the personalities involved and partly through the gradual movement toward more representative government. Before 1688, when James II fled the country and was replaced by his daughter, Mary, and her husband William of Orange, the government was very much the personal affair of the King. After the Great Reform Bill of 1832, regularizing and widening the franchise, it rapidly became the business of ministers and the House of Commons. During the whole of Wilberforce's political life a quiet development toward the latter state of affairs was taking place.

When Wilberforce entered Parliament, the King alone appointed the Prime Ministers and approved most of the others. He formed policy with them as he pleased, and it was well-nigh impossible to pass an important measure to which he was opposed. He could sustain a Prime Minister in office, at least for a time, without a majority in the House of Commons, and could do much, through patronage, threats, and through those who owed their living to him, to ensure that a general election might go his way.

The aristocracy also had great influence—not only because the House of Lords could propose legislation and veto what was passed by the Commons, but also because of the way the House of Commons was elected. Its Members were divided between those representing the counties—two in each case whatever its size—and those representing the boroughs. The electorate in the counties was undoubtedly of a very popular nature. Anyone who was prepared to buy a forty-shilling freehold could obtain a vote. But, in fact, the great land-owning families had great influence, and the allocation of the two county seats was often arranged by negotiation between rival groups of nobles without coming to ballot. This was because, as freeholders would expect bribes and were so numerous, only the richest—at that time the land-owning aristocracy—could afford the expense of an election.

The electorates for the boroughs were infinitely varied. Some, as at Hull, consisted of a third of the population, and, since the law fixed no definite sum to qualify for the franchise, poor men as well as rich, men of the people and members of the middle classes as well as aristocrats, might be included. But there were many "pocket" or "rotten" boroughs. Thus, the Society of the Friends of the People, founded to promote parliamentary reform, estimated in 1793 that fifty-one English and Welsh boroughs whose total electorate was under 1,500 sent 100 representatives and that 11,075 English and Welsh electors returned 257 Members to Parliament. Many of these latter seats were in the gift of rich men or families, generally landed families, though in the last decades of the Eighteenth Century their owners might sell them to the new rich—notably to "nabobs" returning enriched from the West or East Indies or to industrialists who arose during the beginnings of the Industrial Revolution. Dealings of this kind were conducted by borough-mongers or borough-jobbers. In all, however, it must be said that the borough electorate numbered 100,000 people, and was wider than that contemplated by any other European country.

The House of Commons, in fact, did contain many independent Members and, in the ultimate issue, held the power of the purse. It alone could initiate legislation to levy taxes, without which the government could not be carried on. Members were in close touch with public opinion in their districts and public opinion could not, in the end, be ignored. Wilberforce and his friends were among the first to invent methods for bringing its strength to bear upon the Commons and the Government.

There were, at this time, two political parties: the Whigs and the Tories. The Whigs, broadly the aristocratic party, held office continuously from 1714 until 1770. The Tories, then the party more inclined to reform, dated a period of control from the premiership of the Younger Pitt in 1783 and particularly from the election of 1784. But both parties were coalitions of groups centered on individuals or interests more than parties in the modern British sense.

All these circumstances and trends impacted Wilberforce and his times, as we will see in the following pages.

1

The Great Uprooting

TWO HUNDRED YEARS AGO, Britain was the world's leading slave-trading nation. From Liverpool, Bristol or London her ships sailed for the West African coast; and there gathered their cargo by direct seizure, purchase from Arab traders or barter with local chiefs. Often chiefs would sell the entire population of one of their own, or of a neighbour's, villages. The British officials were just as ruthless. Once, a British military governor delivered up a hundred African guests whom he was entertaining in his fort when the slave captains arrived.

Once captured, the slaves were herded into barracoons to await the arrival of the ships. The fit were branded with their new owner's mark, while the old and deformed were often killed as useless. Many had to be flogged to force them into the canoes which took them through the surf to the slave ship. There, they were chained in pairs between decks on shelves with only two and a half feet head-room. A ship of 150 tons often carried as many as 500 slaves. The crew, who had often been press-ganged into service, generally took their pick of the women.

It was obviously in the slaver's interest to keep his cargo in as good health as possible. When weather permitted, therefore, they were taken on deck and forced to jump around under threat of the whip.

In bad weather, on the other hand, they would lie for weeks in their own filth and the stench could be smelled across a mile of ocean. By the time a ship reached America or the West Indies, ten per cent of the cargo would normally have died, while many others would be desperately ill.

On arrival a few days would be spent smartening them up for market. Their bodies were fattened and oiled, their sores disguised. Finally, they would be paraded naked through the streets and auctioned. Strong men would fetch as much as £40, while the sick and wounded were sold off in cheap lots with the women and children. Families were ruthlessly split up. Those who were too sick to be marketable were left on the quay to die. Nor was that the end of their ordeal. A third of those who survived thus far died from the vicious discipline imposed by their new owners. The process was politely known as "seasoning."

The Trade, in which most European countries took part, was dominated by the British. In 1770 British ships carried over half the 100,000 slaves exported from West Africa. Between 1783 and 1793, Liverpool slavers alone transported 303,737 to the West Indies, selling them for £15,186,850 (roughly £250 million at today's values). The profit on the triangular voyage, taking into account goods bartered in Africa and cargo brought back from the West Indies, as well as the price of the slaves, was often over 100 percent of the original outlay, and was widely shared among the inhabitants of the Western ports. "Many of the small ships that carry about a hundred slaves are fitted out by attorneys, drapers, ropers, grocers, barbers, tailors etc. Almost every order of the people is interested in a Guinea cargo," wrote a Liverpudlian in 1795.

The total number of slaves carried by the British in the eighteenth century is hard to estimate, but an American authority calculates that they had supplied three million to the French, Spanish and British colonies by 1776.

For England, indeed, the Trade had become not just another successful business, but national policy. It had not always been so. When she discovered that Sir John Hawkins, the Comptroller and Treasurer of her navy, had earlier made several profitable slaving voyages, Queen Elizabeth was horrified and told him that, if any Africans had been carried away without their own consent, "it would be detestable and call down the vengeance of Heaven on the undertakers." However, this attitude of distaste turned to approval as the profits involved became apparent, and as Britain herself acquired colonies in the Caribbean. The Trade was legalized by Royal Charters of 1631, 1633 and 1672 and by Act of Parliament in 1698. One of the most prized fruits of the War of Spanish Succession was the Assiento clause of the Treaty of Utrecht, giving Britain the sole right to supply slaves to the Spanish Colonies. Meanwhile, "The Institution," as slavery itself was called, was considered "the pillar and support of the British plantation industry in the West Indies."

Moreover, it became part of the conventional wisdom that the Slave Trade was crucial to national security. It provided, it was said, an admirable training for British seamen, and an essential recruiting ground for the British navy. Others declared that it alone made possible the prosperity and even the solvency of the herring and Newfoundland fisheries, and of the sugar refining and shipbuilding and other associated industries.

The national investment involved was certainly considerable. "Abolition," contended Colonel Tarleton, a Member for Liverpool, in 1791, "would instantly annihilate a trade, which annually employed upwards of 5,500 sailors, upwards of 160 ships, and whose exports amount to £800,000 sterling, and would undoubtedly bring the West India trade to decay, whose exports and imports amount to upwards of £6,000,000 sterling, and which give employment to upwards of 160,000 tons of additional shipping, and sailors in proportion." "The present British capital in the West Indies," stated the Duke of

Clarence eight years later, "is equal to £100,000,000 ster-ling."

A trade where so much money and national prestige was involved naturally exercised a good deal of influence in Parliament and in the country. Many planters and traders had used their new wealth to buy "rotten" and "pocket" bor-oughs, which sent themselves or Members controlled by them to the Commons. Thus Lord Chesterfield complained in 1767 that a borough jobber, to whom he had offered £2,500 for a seat, "laughed at" his bid and said that East and West Indian planters were paying anything from £3,000 to £5,000 each. By the end of the century, the Trade controlled a considerable block of seats.

The Trade's main support in Parliament, however, was among the much larger number of Members who, revering property and the status quo, were convinced that the "abso-lute necessity" of slaves to the West Indies meant that the trade could never be discontinued. Few were prepared to meddle with the interests of the West Indian colonists in the years immediately after the loss of the American colonies; and it was felt that if the British ceased to carry slaves, her continental rivals would merely wax rich on her restraint.

Meanwhile, in the country at large, there was widespread ignorance about the conditions which the slaves had to endure. Even people in Bristol and Liverpool, let alone those in the country at large, neither saw the slaves nor experienced the conditions of the Middle Passage between Africa and the Americas. They merely saw the cotton goods with which the ships were loaded and the tropical products they brought back. Moreover, white Englishmen, too, were frequently trans-ported to Australia for petty crimes, and unseen cruelties did not stand out too sharply in an age when inhumanity abounded at home.

A few voices were raised in protest. The Quakers had condemned the Trade as early as 1724 and, in concert with their Pennsylvanian brethren, disowned all Friends taking part in it from 1761. Alexander Pope, John Locke and the non-conformist Divine, Richard Baxter, wrote against it. John Wesley, who quarrelled with George Whitefield about it, produced a widely read pamphlet terming it "the execrable sum of all villainy." Dr. Johnson scandalized his hosts at an Oxford High Table by toasting the next Negro revolt in the West Indies.

The first practical restriction on the evil, however, was the work of a seemingly insignificant clerk in the Government service. Granville Sharp was a brilliant eccentric, gifted with phenomenal intellectual energy and determination. He taught himself Greek so as to be able to confound a colleague on the New Testament, and Hebrew to correct a Rabbi on the Biblical prophesies. He then became convinced that slavery could not legally exist on English soil; and that the 14,000 black slaves then living in Britain should be set free. Every lawyer he consulted, from the great Blackstone downwards, disagreed with him but in 1772 a reluctant Chief Justice Mansfield was forced to endorse his opinion, and the 14,000 slaves were declared free.

Such individual skirmishes had some effect, but it needed the well-publicized atrocity of the slave ship *Zong* in 1783 to rouse a national response. The ship had lost its way in the Middle Passage, sixty slaves and seven crew had died of an epidemic and its supply of water was running low, though not critically so. The ship's captain, realizing that more slaves would die and the rest might make low prices in Jamaica, threw one hundred and thirty two overboard. He reckoned that this could be shown to be for the safety of the ship and that the underwriters would pay compensation. Most of the slaves were thrown overboard shackled, but the last ten broke free and jumped. One of them managed to clamber back on board and survived to tell Granville Sharp his story.

The captain, on his return, was rewarded, but the underwriters brought an action against the ship's owners, which Sharp intended to follow with a criminal prosecution for murder. Even the civil action, however, failed. It was, said the Attorney-General, "a case of goods and chattels," "a throwing of goods overboard to save the residue." The law, added the ever meticulous Chief Justice Mansfield, was "exactly as if horses had been thrown overboard." The Solicitor-General meanwhile deprecated the "pretended appeals" to humanity and agreed that the master had the unquestioned right to drown as many slaves as he thought fit without "any shew or suggestions of cruelty" or any "surmise of impropriety."

It was perhaps the shock of this appalling case which hastened the formation of the first Committee, all Quakers, "for the relief and liberation of the negro slaves in the West Indies and for the discouragement of the Slave Trade on the Coast of Africa." The same year, a book by James Ramsay, a former naval surgeon turned parson, gave the first eye-witness account of the conditions on the Middle Passage and in the plantations. In 1785, Thomas Clarkson, who won a Cambridge University prize with his essay on "Slavery and Commerce in the Human Species" and who was to become the movement's most assiduous researcher, joined the campaign; and two years later the Quaker Committee was enlarged to include Clarkson, and Granville Sharp as Chairman. It was obvious, however, that the real battle would have to be fought out in Parliament and, there, the Abolitionists still lacked an adequate advocate.

As early as 1780 Edmund Burke, the great "political moralist," had considered a measure to mitigate and finally abolish the Trade, but abandoned it for fear that the West Indian lobby would shatter the Whig Party. Nor did Pitt, the new young Prime Minister, dare to lead such a fight against the opposition of both the King and most of his Cabinet. Any politician who took up the issue would clearly have to say farewell to the chance of high office, yet be weighty enough to capture the attention of the great. He would need to be orator enough to arouse the pity and disgust of the House, and to have the determination to pursue a cause, year after year, the intelligence to master a complicated subject and the charm to disarm prejudice, where he could not dispel it. Where could such a man be found?

In fact, he was in the House of Commons already, and being prepared in more ways than one. In October 1780, at the age of twenty-one, William Wilberforce had taken his seat as Member for Hull, just three months before his Cambridge contemporary, William Pitt. The two young men became close friends and, while Pitt became first, Chancellor of the Exchequer and then Prime Minister, Wilberforce won for himself one of the two seats for Yorkshire, the greatest county of England. Meanwhile, too, something even stranger had befallen Wilberforce, something which would dispose him to espouse a great cause. To understand that timely coincidence we must go back and see what manner of young man he was.

2

Hull Boy Makes Good

WILLIAM WILBERFORCE WAS BORN in Hull, the fourth port of the Kingdom, and the only one of the four not engaged in the Slave Trade. Facing east, she thrived on the older Baltic Trade, importing Swedish ore, Norwegian timber and Russian hemp, and shipping back Sheffield knives and Yorkshire textiles. It was also a major whaling port. The Wilberforces had been well-known traders in nearby Beverley for two hundred years, but William's grandfather moved to Hull at the beginning of the century, became Mayor at the age of 32 and was, by the time of William's birth, established in a fine red-brick house in High Street, with his back windows looking out on the Hull River which carried his trade.

Hull did not give rise to men of spectacular wealth like Bristol or Liverpool. Its gaieties, which some considered second only to London's, ensured that many of the West Riding county families kept town houses there, but it was run by an oligarchy of solid mercantile families of whom the Wilberforces were one. William's grandfather had married into the Thorntons, another prosperous Baltic Trade family, and his elder son, another William, married his first cousin, Hannah Thornton, and joined his father-in-law in London, where he plied a sizable trade with Russia and was also a director of the Bank of England. Robert, the younger son and our William's father, managed the business in Hull, together with a partner, Abel Smith, and they married two sisters. Abel came from a Nottingham banking family, and founded banks in Hull and London which were ancestors of the present National Westminster, one of the largest banks in Britain today. So young William was born into comfortable circumstances and a strong mercantile and banking tradition.

He was a weak child, tiny, frail, and with the poor eyesight which plagued him all his life. He often said in later life that, had he been born "in less civilized times"—and he might have added less comfortable circumstances—it would have been thought impossible to rear him. But if his body was weak, his mind was vigorous, his nature affectionate and his temper, at times, hot. He also had a voice of unusual range and beauty, and his headmaster at Hull Grammar School, Joseph Milner, would stand him on a table to read to the rest of the class, because of his small size and clarity of diction.

William's stay there was brief, however. When he was nine his father died and he went to live with his childless uncle and aunt, William and Hannah Wilberforce, who had a town house in St. James's Place and a country villa on Wimbledon Common.

They sent him to a boarding school in Putney where he learnt little, but, in the holidays, he absorbed a great deal from his uncle and aunt. They were friends of George Whitefield, one of the Wesleys' first recruits to the Holy Club in Oxford and the third great figure of their awakening. Whitefield's more dramatic preaching had made a deeper impression on the wealthier classes than John Wesley's plainer manner and he had, in 1754, converted Hannah's half-brother, John Thornton, one of the most prosperous men in the city. John Thornton lived in Clapham, and Hannah often took William to hear the evangelical sermons preached in the parish church there. His heart was won by what he heard, and particularly by the sermons and stories of the Reverend John Newton, a former slave ship captain who was a frequent visitor to Clapham. "I reverenced him as a parent when I was a child," William said later in life.

William's mother, at home in Hull, became thoroughly alarmed by her son's letters, fearing that he was "turning Methodist." She was religious in a formal sense, but loved social life in the "Dublin of England" and had the fashionable hatred of "enthusiasm." She took the coach to London to rescue her only son from what she considered "little less than poison," while Grandfather Wilberforce vowed that "if Billy turns Methodist he shall not have a sixpence of mine." William's uncle and aunt protested, but his mother blandly replied, "You should not fear. If it be a work of grace, you cannot fail," and bore William away to Hull. Since Joseph Milner was by now also suspected of "Methodism," he was not returned to the Grammar School as headmaster but, instead, dispatched to his grandfather's old school at Pocklington, thirty miles away.

William felt the parting from his aunt and uncle deeply. "It almost broke my heart," he said later, and his letters to them over the next three years show that this was one of the unhappiest periods of his life. The letters are full of his lonely struggles to retain his faith in the face of a concerted opposition from his home and his new headmaster, the Reverend K. Basket. They had to be written in secret. "P.S. I cannot write more because it is seen where the letter is to," he concludes one note in November 1771, and in September of the following year explains that he is taking, "the opportunity of writing by a maid who goes away tomorrow: thinking it the better way than sending to my uncle, since grandpa might perhaps see the letter."

Meanwhile the gaieties of Hull were gradually having their effect on his naturally vivacious spirit. "The theatre, balls, great suppers and card parties were the delight of the principal families of the town," he wrote later. "The usual dinner hour was two o'clock, and at six they met for sumptuous suppers. This mode of life was at first distressing to me, but by degrees I acquired a relish for it . . . As grandson of one of the principal inhabitants, I was everywhere invited and caressed: my voice and love of music made me still more acceptable. The religious impressions which I gained at Wimbledon continued for a considerable time, but my friends spared no pains to stifle them. I might almost say that no pious parent ever laboured more to impress a beloved child with sentiments of piety than they did to give me a taste of the world and its diversions."

By 1774, to judge from his letters, the social whirl had captured him and, in spite of the pain he had gone through, Wilberforce was later to reflect that it might all have been a "blessing in disguise." His mother's removing him "when about thirteen and then completely a Methodist, has probably been the means of my being connected with political men and becoming useful in life," he wrote when 37. "If I had staid with my uncle I should probably have become a bigoted and despised Methodist; yet to come to what I am now, after so many years of folly as those which elapsed between my last year at school and 1785, is wonderful."

The "idle life at home" and the social success which had made him "very vain" did not dispose him to much academic exertion either at Pocklington or at St. John's College, Cambridge, which he entered in 1776 at the age of seventeen.

His grandfather's death two years earlier had supplied him with ample funds, and he settled easily into eighteenth-century Cambridge where dons were content that young men of independent means, if not studying for the Church or the Bar, should treat the university as a place to gather a little culture, together with a trifling acquaintance with mathematics and the classics.

"The first night I arrived," he wrote, "I supped with my tutor and was introduced to two of the most gambling, vicious characters perhaps in all England." In his second year, he broke with this group and lived much with the Fellows in a state of what he called "sober dissipation." "I used to play at cards a great deal and nothing else." He added, "If ever I became studious they said to me, 'Why in the world should a man of your future trouble himself with fagging?'" However, he had a natural love of the classics and managed, with little work and a good memory, to pass his examinations, though not with honours.

His neighbour, Thomas Gisborne, who was to become a life-long friend, was reading for holy orders. He won the Chancellor's medal for Classics and was Sixth Wrangler in Mathematics. Flatterers said, in Wilberforce's hearing, that "Gisborne is very clever, but he fags, whereas Wilberforce can do as much without working at all." It was not true, and Wilberforce always regretted afterwards that he had not acquired the disciplined concentration of a Gisborne.

Wilberforce was naturally gregarious and soon became extremely popular. "By his talents, his wit, his kindness, his social powers, his universal acceptability, and his love of society, he speedily became the centre of attraction to all the clever and idle of his own college and of other colleges," Gisborne wrote in old age. "His rooms swarmed with them from the time when he rose, generally very late, till he went to bed . . . He spent much of his time visiting, and when he returned late in the evening he would summon me by the music of his tongs and poker—our chimneypieces being back to back—or by the melodious challenge of his voice. He was so winning and amusing that I often sat up half the night with him, much to the detriment of my attendance of lectures the next day." Wilberforce always kept a vast Yorkshire pie in his room to regale his many guests, among whom, says Gisborne, he was *facile princeps.*

Others of Wilberforce's Cambridge companions, men like the feckless Rutland landowner Gerard Edwards, also became life-long friends, but Wilberforce saw little of young William Pitt although they were contemporaries. They first got to know each other well in the gallery of the House of Commons where, immediately after going down from Cambridge, they listened to the debates night after night. For Wilberforce, like

Pitt, had decided to make politics his career. The death of his Wimbledon uncle brought him a substantial legacy and his cousin, Abel Smith, was more than happy to run the business in Hull; so he was free to do so. Pitt was powered by a deeper motive. He was possessed by a smouldering bitterness against the American War which had done so much to wreck his father's work. So the two young men longed for an election, but not too soon, for no one could "stand" for Parliament under the age of 21. Fortunately, the Government survived the necessary months, and Pitt stood for Cambridge, while Wilberforce threw his cap into the ring in Hull.

He was, of course, well known there, but it was a bold ambition for so young a man. Hull had one of the twenty largest borough electorates in Britain, with about 1,100 electors in a population of 15,000. It was a two-Member seat and each elector had two votes. Traditionally, the Government of the day could secure the return of one member through the votes of the garrison (soldiers stationed in Hull) and excise officers (customs and tax officials working at this large port). Their man for thirty-three years, who intended to stand again, was Lord Robert Manners, uncle of the Duke of Rutland. The great Whig families, headed by the Marquess of Rockingham, generally returned the other Member, who was then David Hartley, a dull speaker, an opponent of the American war and something of an eccentric. He may have been the first person to speak seriously to Wilberforce about the evils of the slave trade.

The mass of the electors were hereditary freemen, generally "persons of low station" who required a bribe. The going rate for a resident freeman was two guineas a vote, or four for a "plumper," when an elector voted for one candidate but did not exercise his second vote. An elector who had to travel from London, on the other hand, could expect £10. It was, of course, their ample means which gave the great Whig families their power, but on this occasion, Wilberforce's charm and purse, supplemented by an ox roast for the town at large on his twenty-first birthday, enabled him to beat both the Government and Rockingham factions. He secured 1,126 votes, exactly the number obtained by the other two candidates added together. It had cost him £8,000.

So Wilberforce and Manners were elected. Pitt, meanwhile, had been defeated at Cambridge, but entered Parliament three months later for the "rotten borough" of Appleby, made available to him by the great Northern borough-monger, Sir James Lowther.

3

"The Foinsters"

A STILL GREATER TEST now awaited Wilberforce. He may have won Hull, where he was well known; he had not yet won his way into the close-knit web of London society, where, as he recalled later, he "knew not a single person above the rank of commoner, scarcely a merchant." Yet acceptance into the exclusive clubs of St. James's and the great country houses was essential for a successful political career, and so he approached London with some trepidation.

He need not have worried. As a young, rich and charming Member of Parliament, doors opened to him readily enough. He was amusing, his mimicry of the Prime Minister Lord North soon became famous, and his voice was so sweet that he became known as the Nightingale of the House of Commons. The Prince of Wales, after listening to him sing at the Duchess of Devonshire's ball in 1782, said he would go anywhere to hear him. "When I left the House," wrote the celebrated man-about-town, George Selwyn, that same year, "I left in one room a party of young men who made me, for their life and spirits, wish for one night to be twenty. There was a table full of them drinking—young Pitt, Lord Euston, Berkeley, etc., singing and laughing à *gorge employée*; some of them sang very good snatches; one Wilberforce, a MP, sang the best."

The clubs fulfilled three purposes. They were political societies, social meeting places and casinos. White's was the main Tory watering-hole, while Brooks', on the opposite side of St. James's, was the Whig stronghold. As an independent, Wilberforce became a member of both, though it took him longer to penetrate Brooks' where, incidentally, the stakes at the tables were highest. He also joined Boodle's—winning twenty-five guineas from the Duke of Norfolk his first evening there—and several other clubs. He enjoyed gaming, but never became an addict like Charles James Fox, who had lost £140,000 before he was twenty-four or the Duchess of Devonshire who is said to have parted with over a million pounds. For Wilberforce added a certain Yorkshire shrewdness to his ardour and, to both, a remnant of conscience. He gave up the devastating game of faro when, after winning six hundred pounds in an evening, he found those most heavily hit were young men who had not yet entered into their fortunes.

His favourite haunt, and Pitt's too, was Goosetrees. Twenty-five Cambridge contemporaries had taken over a club of that name in Pall Mall and Wilberforce and Pitt dined there almost every night when they were in town. There other friendships mellowed too, particularly with Edward Eliot, who was to marry Pitt's sister Harriot, with Henry Bankes, the Member for Dorset, with Pepper Arden, and Grenville as well as with Gerard Edwards, late of St. John's College.

Wilberforce also loved the general stir of society. He patronized the opera and the theatres, and delighted in the art and company of Mrs. Siddons. The lovely Duchess of Gordon, who was rumoured to have recruited the Gordon Highlanders by giving each applicant a shilling from her lips, was a frequent visitor to his house. And, in spite of his small frame, he thought nothing of walking for five hours, and then drinking far into the night at Goosetrees.

Once, after dining with Henry Dundas, Pitt's mainstay in
Scotland, he stayed talking the whole night through, as if back
in Cambridge. We are even told by Macaulay, the historian,
that, at one period, Wilberforce took tea each evening in a
brothel. This information, imparted to him at a largish breakfast party by Wilberforce's son, Samuel, then Bishop of
Oxford, greatly surprised Macaulay. The Bishop had made it
clear that these visits were not for licentious purposes, but
because it was the fashion among young men. "I should have
kept the secret from my son if I had been Wilberforce senior
and from the public if I had been Wilberforce junior," Macaulay commented in his diary.

Yet underneath the modishness and the soaring ambition,
Wilberforce's friends seemed to detect a deeper note than in
other young men-about-town. "I thank God," Gerard Edwards wrote in 1782, "that I live in the age of Wilberforce and
that I know one man at least who is both moral and entertaining." Moral, Wilberforce would certainly not have called
himself, except perhaps that he had avoided the sexual liaisons
so common among his contemporaries.

Pitt, meanwhile, was making rapid strides. His maiden
speech in the House, on financial reform, was a sensation. It
caused Fox to put him up immediately for membership of
Brooks' and Wilberforce to exclaim, "I doubt not that I shall,
one day or another, see him the first man in the country." In
June, Pitt followed up with a brilliant attack on the American
War, in the spirit of his father and, in December, with another
on the same subject. Six months later, at the age of twenty-
three, after being in the House only eighteen months, he was
appointed Chancellor of the Exchequer in Lord Shelburne's
administration.

Wilberforce's first speeches were pedestrian efforts on
local Hull affairs. It was not until 1782, with Shelburne and Pitt
out of power and Lord North in office again, that he entered
the larger arena, telling Ministers that they were acting more
like lunatics than statesmen and that they had conducted the
American War in a "cruel, bloody and impractical way." North

fell, Rockingham came in briefly, to be succeeded by Shelburne, who ended the War. He, in turn, gave way to a
coalition headed by Fox, Burke, North and Portland. It was
now that Wilberforce made his name, with his darting repartee
and devastating sarcasm. For Fox to join North, the target so
long of his tremendous denunciations, seemed to Wilberforce
the height of absurdity, and he was not slow to say so.

Meanwhile, during Shelburne's administration, Lauriston
House, the Wimbledon villa which Wilberforce had inherited
from his uncle, came into its own. It had been his to use since
1777, but now this ample Surrey retreat, with its eight
bedrooms and standing in 3 1/2 acres of garden, teemed with
life. In the spring and summer, Pitt preferred to sleep there
than at Downing Street and would ride out after work or when
the House rose, even if that meant "taking to horse" after
midnight. "Eliot, Arden and I will be with you before curfew
and expect an early meal of peas and strawberries," wrote Pitt
in one note to Wilberforce.

Here, among old friends, the grave young Minister could
relax. One morning, he was found to have been up early
cutting the opera hat of his future Foreign Secretary, Dudley
Ryder, into pieces and sowing them in the flower beds. And a
lieutenant of Shelburne's complained that, his lordship being
out of town, he had been unable to talk with Pitt who:

> passes, as usual, most of his time with his young Friends in a
> Society very lively—some little excess happen'd lately at
> Wimbledon . . . In the Evening some of the Neighbours were
> alarmed with noises at their doors, but Nobody, I believe,
> has made any ill natured reflection upon a mere frolic—It has
> only been pleasantly remarked, that the Rioters were headed
> by Mr. P, later Chancellor of the Ex-, and Master Arden, late
> Solicitor Genl.

The young men's favourite pastime was what they called

foining* (jesting and "ragging and exchanging witty repar-
tees"), and Edward Eliot called their intimate circle "the
foinsters." Wilberforce's effervescent wit was here readily
displayed, while Wilberforce thought Pitt at this time "the
wittiest man he ever knew." "All the others seemed to say a
witty thing just as it arose from the collision as it were of the
steel with the flint . . . Mr. Pitt was systematically witty," he
wrote, long afterwards. "The others were often run away with
by their wit. Mr. Pitt was always master of his."

Pitt badly needed this escape from his serious nature. He
was a somewhat forbidding figure, a man set aside from
childhood by inheritance and intellect for high office. He was
less expert at handling people than ideas. His shyness—"I am
the shyest man alive," he once told Wilberforce—made him
seem cold and arrogant. He did not make friends easily, nor
lose them when made, for those close to him, like Wilberforce,
regarded him as the sum of all the human virtues.

Pitt appreciated what Wimbledon gave him. "Adieu, I
must conclude, having no time for foining," ends one note to
Wilberforce.

On another occasion, Wilberforce wrote to him: "You
may reckon yourself most fortunate in that cheerfulness of
mind which enables you every now and then to throw off your
load for a few hours. I fancy it must be this which, when I am
with you, prevents me considering you an object of compassion, tho' Prime Minister of England, for now, when I am out
of hearing of your foyning . . . I cannot help representing you
to myself as oppressed with cares and troubles."

In fact, their characters were complementary. Wilberforce
had the vivacity, gregariousness and perception of character
which Pitt lacked, together with the sensitiveness which knew
at any moment what his friend needed. That was why, at

---

*Foining or foyning: a common eighteenth-century term: contesting (physically or
verbally).

Wimbledon, Pitt could indulge in practical jokes or burst out singing in a way which would have astonished Whitehall.

It was natural that the two should become great friends. Often, indeed, they were alone at Wimbledon. "For weeks and months together I spent hours with him every morning while he transacted business . . . Hundreds of times, probably, I have called him out of bed and conversed with him while he was dressing. I was the depository of his most confidential thoughts," said Wilberforce years later. Pitt used the house as his own for some four years.

In September 1783, the two of them, with Eliot, met at Bankes' house in Dorset and then crossed to France together. In Paris they met Benjamin Franklin and Lafayette. At Fontainebleau, Wilberforce was bewitched by Marie Antoinette and thought Louis XVI, in his clumsy boots, a being strange enough to come a hundred miles to see. The trip ended suddenly in late October when a messenger urged Pitt's immediate return to England, followed two days later by his friends.

The Fox-North Coalition was still riding high, but Fox's India Bill, yet another attempt to find a less corrupt way of running the East India Company and its vast possessions in India, seemed to be vesting such enormous powers of patronage in the Government that Pitt and Wilberforce threw themselves into the debate against it with all their strength. Much of the City, together with the merchants and squires, who in political terms then constituted "the people," were also alarmed, and the King, who loathed Fox as much for his corruption of the Prince of Wales' morals as for his politics, was looking for a chance to get rid of him. The Bill passed the Commons, but was thrown out in the Lords through the direct intervention of the Sovereign. Next day, on December 18th, the King dismissed the Coalition and Pitt, at the age of twenty-four, became Prime Minister in a hostile House.

At first the news caused disbelief and the young Premier had difficulty in forming a Government. He eventually succeeded, but every Minister except himself was in the House of

Lords, and he was more than ever reliant on Wilberforce, now perhaps his only supporter of real eloquence in the Commons. So the two friends, matched in age and complementary in brilliance, set out on the hazardous road together.

Never before or since has a British Prime Minister been so young. Yet it was an age of youth. George III himself had succeeded to the throne at twenty-three, Nelson had been gazetted post-captain at twenty and Wellington, like Clive before him, won his Indian victories at a ridiculously early age by modern standards. The stakes were high, but the opportunities unlimited.

4

Member for Yorkshire

IN THE FIRST THREE months of 1784, Pitt's motions were constantly defeated in the House, but the King retained him in office. This unconstitutional situation, however, could not go on indefinitely. Sooner or later Parliament would have to be dissolved.

Wilberforce began to harbour his most audacious ambition yet—to stand as one of the two Members for the county of Yorkshire. Yorkshire was both the largest and most important of the counties and, up to that time, no member of the mercantile class had ever wrested a county seat from the control of the great landed families. The two Yorkshire Members represented the entire county, except for the city of York and thirteen older boroughs like Hull; and, since the new industrial towns of Leeds, Bradford, Halifax and Sheffield had no separate representation, the county Members spoke for the manufacturers and the artisans as well as the squires and yeomen of the countryside. Sir George Saville who, with Henry Duncombe, had represented the county until his death in 1783 called it "a little kingdom."

Because of the vast expense of an election in this enormous constituency, with its 20,000 scattered voters, the great landed magnates had always been able to arrange the nomination of candidates among themselves, while being careful, of course, not to put forward anyone whom the squires and mercantile men actively disliked. Indeed, in the century before the Reform Bill of 1832, only four Yorkshire elections, those of 1734, 1741, 1807 and 1830, ever went to the polls, for the cost of bribing and cajolling the 12,000 votes needed to obtain a majority in a contested election was at least £100,000, the equivalent of £1,500,000 today. What generally happened was that extensive soundings were undertaken by both sides, and, on the basis of their "canvasses," they then agreed whether to share the seats between them or yield both seats to the other party.

In 1779, however, a new influence had arisen in the county with the founding of the Yorkshire Association, dedicated to parliamentary reform and led by a landed clergyman called Christopher Wyvill. Wyvill now saw Pitt as the best hope of Reform and was eager to have an immediate election at which he hoped two Pittite Members would be elected. He decided to try and force the issue by collecting sufficient signatures to require the High Sheriff of the county to summon a general meeting of Yorkshire freeholders who would then consider an Address to the King asking for an election. This was to be held in the grassy yard of York Castle on March 25th, 1784, and the Whig magnates, headed by Lord Fitzwilliam, were determined to secure the rejection of Wyvill's petition since such a rejection, coming from Yorkshire, would, they felt, be disastrous for the young Prime Minister. It was widely assumed that they would succeed.

On March 21st, Wilberforce took a coach for York to do what he could for Pitt, but also harbouring the private ambition which he had not confided even to Pitt. The difficulties in the way of that ambition were far greater even than the winning of the two seats for Pitt. In London, his personality had won him his way into society, but he was little known county-wide in

Yorkshire and, in any case, the landed gentry generally despised the sons of tradesmen, as they would have categorized him. Moreover, there was no obvious vacancy. The county's two Members, the Pittite Duncombe and the Whig Foljambe who had succeeded his uncle, Saville, were both standing; Duncombe would be the first choice of the Pittites and, in the event of a compromise, Foljambe seemed likely to be put in by the Fitzwilliam interest. Even if the Pittites won both seats, Wilberforce's candidature was in no one's mind but his own.

Arriving on March 24th, Wilberforce lodged with his only real friend in York, a Canon of the Minster, and the two of them helped Wyvill, whom Wilberforce knew only slightly, to draft the Address to be put before the meeting next day.

Thursday March 25th was bitterly cold, windy with hail storms. The Whig magnates arrived in carriages with their retinues; the Duke of Devonshire with his brother, Sir John Cavendish, the Member for York; Lord Surrey, the Duke of Norfolk's heir; and a posse of Earls and lesser noblemen headed by Lord Fitzwilliam. In all, four thousand freeholders came pouring into what the *York Chronicle* described as "a more numerous and respectable (audience) than any ever held on a similar occasion." Everyone there possessed a country estate or mercantile wealth. Only two noblemen, Effingham and Faulconburg, were known to be inclined towards Pitt and the King.

From mid-morning till late afternoon, the debate continued. Twelve long speeches were delivered, mostly against the Address, and the audience were tiring when, around 4 p.m., the diminutive figure of Wilberforce, five feet, four inches high and a mere thirty-three inches round the chest, briskly mounted the wooden table from which the speeches were being made. The weather was by now so bad that an eye-witness thought that his slight frame "would be unable to make head against its violence." Few knew him even by sight, but his magnificent voice carried easily to the furthest corners of the crowd. A newspaper reported: "Mr. Wilberforce made a most argumentative and eloquent speech, which was listened to with the most eager attention, and received with the loudest acclamations of applause. It was indeed a reply to everything that had been said against the Address; but there was such an exquisite choice of expression, and pronounced with such rapidity, that we are unable to do it justice in any account we can give. . . ."

James Boswell, who happened to be there, shivering in the rain, on his way south to see the aged Samuel Johnson, gave a more picturesque account a few days later to Henry Dundas: "I saw a little fellow on a table speaking, a perfect shrimp. But presently the shrimp swelled into a whale." Wilberforce, said High Sheriff Danby, "spoke like an angel."

He had been on his feet for nearly an hour, when a King's Messenger, who had ridden post-haste from London, pushed his way through the crowd. Wilberforce paused, read a letter and then, abandoning his theme, dramatically announced, on Pitt's authority, for the letter was from him, that Parliament had been dissolved that very day. "We have now," continued Wilberforce, "to decide upon a solemn crisis: you are now upon trial; we have heard much of an Aristocracy; if there is any such bias in your minds, let no little consideration weigh against the public interest. If you approve those Ministers who have fought, and, I hope I shall say, have conquered, in support of the Constitution, come forth and honestly say so. . . ." Amid cries of "We'll have this man for our county Member," Lord John Cavendish, the last speaker, made no headway and the Address was carried by acclamation.

This, of course, still did not mean that Wilberforce had won himself the Pittite nomination with Duncombe, let alone assured his election to Parliament. That night, as the Pittite forces celebrated their victory, many drinking too well, the inherent rivalries in the camp broke into violent quarrelling. Wilberforce and Wyvill managed to restore harmony, and, as the party broke up at midnight, Wilberforce got to his feet and said he could now sleep easy since their triumph was not spoilt by internal division. "Bravo, little Wilberforce," shouted Harry

Pierse of Bedale impulsively. "I tell you what. I will give £500 towards bringing you in for the county!" The room echoed with cries of "Wilberforce for ever! Wilberforce and Liberty!"

Next morning, when the Pittites met, heads were cooler and many spoke of the expense of a contest. A young man named Richard Milnes interrupted. "We have £10,000 in this room alone," he shouted and, when the rival party sent word suggesting the compromise of a Pittite and a Foxite, the sitting members in fact, it was contemptuously rejected. All the Pittites united behind Duncombe and Wilberforce. And, after a ten-day canvass by each side, this combination proved so strong that the Foxites decided that a county poll would be an expensive waste of time. Lord Fitzwilliam considered that he was "not deserted by the better part of the county, but beat by the ragamuffins," but Wilberforce's diary reads: "Up early. Breakfasted tavern—rode frisky horse to castle—elected—chaired—dined York Tavern. Spencer Stanhope (his successor in Hull) spoke for me."

He returned to London a hero, for, as Fox always maintained, it was the Yorkshire victory which had "set the tone" for the country. The election had not cost Wilberforce a penny and only a quarter of the fund of £18,670 raised by his supporters had been needed. Pitt carried the country by a landslide.

5

The "Great Change"

As MEMBER FOR YORKSHIRE, Wilberforce had now become a man of consequence in his own right. Winning, against such odds, the most coveted seat in Parliament set him in a position immediately after that of Cabinet Ministers and the leaders of the Opposition in importance, a position buttressed, too, by his intimate friendship with the Prime Minister and by his debating skills. A Yorkshire Foxite averred that Wilberforce's whole aim had been so to triumph as to force from Pitt some lucrative office to repair his allegedly strained finances, and, indeed, two elections (he had stood for Hull simultaneously with Yorkshire as an insurance policy) had made a sizable hole in his pocket. The financial situation was not, in fact, either urgent or uppermost in Wilberforce's mind.

He would certainly have welcomed office, but none came, no doubt because Pitt had too many debts to pay to less committed allies. Almost all of his Cabinet were again, in fact, in the Lords. "A little pressure," writes Warner, "must have brought him [Wilberforce] almost any post for which he asked." In dealing with Pitt, however, Wilberforce's ambitions were tempered by the delicacy of friendship. "He knows I would never ask anything of him," he had noted on an earlier occasion.

Meanwhile, his debating powers were at Pitt's disposal, and they had become considerable. Pitt said that he possessed "the greatest natural eloquence of all the men I ever knew," which was no light assessment from so great an orator in that age of orators. The phrase was exactly chosen. Wilberforce did not contrive or even always prepare his speeches in detail. He used a conversational style, quite different from the exquisitely turned phrases of a Burke or a Windham.* The unique qualities of his voice were a part of it. His diction, wrote a Parliamentary reporter, "was so distinct and melodious that the most hostile ear hangs on them delighted. Then his address is so insinuating that if he talked nonsense you would feel obliged to hear him." His warmth of feeling moved Members' hearts as well as their heads, and he was master of a devastating sarcasm, little used later on, but at full throttle in the Parliament of 1784. Pitt so valued him that he once offered to postpone the meeting of Parliament for ten days rather than face the session without him.

So, in 1784, Wilberforce stood at a pinnacle of achievement. At twenty-four, he had won an unassailable position both in politics and society. Office could not long be delayed, and the future was bright with opportunities. Life, too, was infinitely enjoyable. He was privy to most Cabinet secrets and welcome in all the grandest houses. It was at this moment that a series of events took place which were to transform his prospects. They shattered his aims, and left him a new man but uncertain of his destiny.

The process began when he took his mother and sister Sally to spend the winter on the Franco-Italian Riviera because of Sally's health. They took with them Sally's delicate cousin,

---

*Orator and Secretary of State for War in George Grenville's Government, circa 1763–5. Grenville passed the fatal Stamp Act for taxing American colonies.

Bessy Smith, and Wilberforce invited Isaac Milner, the brother of his former Hull headmaster and now a tutor at Cambridge, to come along as male companion. Milner accepted, and they set out in two carriages, the women in a coach and the men in a post-chaise. They must have looked a strange pair in that post-chaise: tiny, effervescent Wilberforce and Milner, "the most enormous man it was ever my fate to see in a drawing room," as Marianne Thornton was to describe him.

Milner, since they had met briefly when he was master at Hull, had developed into a massive intellect, versatile if sometimes a little ponderous. After a few years' teaching at the Grammar School, he had gone to Cambridge where he came first in the mathematics examinations with the word *incomparabilis* after his name. By now, he combined a membership of the Royal Society with his fellowship at Queen's College. Later, he was to hold the Cambridge chairs of both Natural Philosophy and Mathematics, and to be both President of Queen's and Vice-Chancellor of the University.

At this point, Wilberforce records that, although a clergyman, Milner was "very much a man of the world in his manners and . . . lively and dashing in his conversation," with no sign of the Evangelical influence of his brother Joseph. Wilberforce would never have invited an Evangelical, for the influence of his Wimbledon uncle and aunt was now well buried and he thought such views were only held by "vulgar or at least uninformed enthusiastic persons." His favourite preacher was Theophilus Lindsey, the "father" of modern Unitarianism, in whose Essex Street chapel he kept a sitting. Lindsey still preached the Christian ethic, but had abandoned belief in the divinity of Christ.

The party crossed the Channel on October 20th, 1784, and in the chaise across France Wilberforce ridiculed, with all his bitter skill, the views of "Methodists" such as his aunt and her brother John Thornton, the banker. He also propounded some of Lindsey's Unitarian ideas, condemning the Christian view of the Atonement and the authority of Scripture.

Milner, in contrast to his habitual jocularity, replied gravely: "Wilberforce, I don't pretend to be match for you in this sort of running fire. But if you really wish to discuss these topics in a serious and argumentative manner I shall be most happy to enter into them with you." While there was nothing in Milner's behaviour to suggest that he was a "serious" Christian, he had a firm grasp of the intellectual case for Christianity and was famed for his skill in making complicated matters clear to his students. These he employed in the ensuing debate, but made little visible impact during the journey to Nice.

At Nice, Wilberforce idly picked up a book of his cousin Bessy's, *The Rise and Progress of Religion in the Soul* by Philip Doddridge, and asked Milner what he thought of it. "It is one of the best books ever written," replied Milner, and he suggested that they read it together as they journeyed home for the new Parliamentary session, leaving the ladies behind at Nice. This study, punctuated by frequent reference to passages from the Bible and much discussion, brought Wilberforce to an intellectual assent to Biblical Christianity by the time Milner deposited him at 10 Downing Street on February 22nd, 1785.

Once there, however, he pushed religion to the back of his mind and resumed his social and political pursuits. He was mainly working with Pitt on the Prime Minister's personal Bill to disenfranchise thirty-six rotten boroughs, and give the seats vacated to London and the Counties. "At Pitt's all day—it goes well—sat up late chatting with Pitt—his good hopes for the country, and noble, patriotic heart," reads Wilberforce's journal. And again, "To town—Pitt's—House—Parliamentary Reform—terribly disappointed and beat—extremely fatigued—spoke extremely ill but commended." He dined with Pitt two or three times a week and once "sitting up all night singing—shirked Duchess of Gordon, at Almack's—danced till five in the morning."

The following June, Milner and he set out once more for the Continent to collect the ladies, who had now moved on to Genoa. This time, they read and discussed the New Testament in Greek. The discussion continued on the return journey,

Wilberforce urging his "various doubts, objections and difficulties," which Milner answered one by one. Gradually, intellectual assent developed into deep inner conviction.

In early September, the party paused at the fashionable Belgian resort of Spa which was full of Wilberforce's society friends. He joined in the fun with all his old abandon. True, he would not go to the theatre or travel on Sundays, but he danced, sang glees and snatches and ate and drank himself through enormous meals and social occasions. The thought pressed in upon him, however, that "in the true sense of the word I am no Christian." Unseen by the crowd, a sharp conflict raged inside him. He had begun to question the propriety of his own behaviour.

It was here at Spa that he began his life-long practice of rising early and spending the first hours of the day in meditation. "Began three or four days ago to get up very early," he writes on October 25th. "In the solitude and self-conversation of the morning some thoughts which I trust will come to something." Soon he was overcome with spiritual anguish. "As soon as I recollected seriously, the deep guilt and black ingratitude of my past life forced itself on me in the strongest colours, and I condemned myself for having wasted precious time, and opportunities and talents." It was this "shapeless idleness" which appalled him. And such heart-searchings were to last long after he got back to London. "It was not so much the fear of punishment by which I was affected, as a sense of my great sinfulness in having so long neglected the unspeakable mercies of my God and Saviour." And again, "I was filled with sorrow. I am sure no human being could suffer more than I did for some months."

The struggle was sharp, as it must be for anyone who, for the first time, honestly reviews his life and motives in the light of Christ's demands, and sometimes during this period Wilberforce feared for his reason, while outwardly keeping company with as much gaiety as ever. This crisis, writes John Pollock, "bears the stamp of a classic Christian tradition. Again and again the rebirth of a soul in confrontation with Christ has involved pangs of spirit—Augustine, Luther, Cromwell, Pascal: each refers to darkness preceding the dawn."

Wilberforce reached Wimbledon on November 10th, his mind still in turmoil. On November 21st, he began a private journal, quite distinct from his diary, to record his thoughts as they came each morning. "Great changes are easier than small ones," a quotation from Bacon, is his first entry. In the next days, among many reappraisals of his way of life, he set down thoughts which required action. One was how to order his meditations. Another to "open himself to Pitt." A third, which came persistently and was strongly resisted, was to "go and converse with Mr. [John] Newton."

These thoughts really crystallized his inner battle. If he was to become a Christian, he must be fully at God's command. Would that mean his losing his friends, of whom Pitt was the most valued, and his popularity, laying aside his political and social ambitions? He had to choose between Christ and the world. Like the poet Francis Thompson, he was "sore adread, lest, having Him, he might have naught beside."

The way with Pitt opened first. He called at Wimbledon on November 24th and Wilberforce noted: "Heard the Bible read two hours. Pascal one and a half. Business the same. Pitt called, and commended Butler's *Analogy*—resolved to write to him and discover to him what I am occupied about." In his letter, he told Pitt of his changed view of life, adding that he intended to withdraw from public life for a time. He said he would always "feel strong affection" for Pitt and that he saw no likelihood of their differing seriously in politics, but it was unlikely that he could be "so much a party man" as hitherto. He concluded by suggesting that, when they next met, the letter should not be mentioned, as he dreaded argument about matters which he felt could not be argued.

Pitt's long reply, sent from Downing Street on December 2nd, was serious and full of affection:

As to any public conduct which your opinion may ever lead you to [he wrote] I will not disguise to you that few things could go nearer my heart than to find myself differing from you on any great principle. I trust and believe that it is a circumstance which can hardly occur. But if ever it should, and even if I should experience as much pain in such an event as I have hitherto encouragement and pleasure in the reverse, believe me it is impossible that it should shake the sentiments of affection and friendship which I bear towards you, and which I must be forgetful and insensible indeed if I ever could part with. They are sentiments engraved on my heart, and will never be effaced or weakened. . . .

Coming to Wilberforce's intention of withdrawing from public life, Pitt continued:

You will not suspect me of thinking lightly of any moral or religious motives which guide you. But forgive me if I cannot help expressing my fear that you are deluding yourself into principles which have but too much tendency to counteract your own object, and to render your virtues and your talents useless both to yourself and to mankind.

Solitude could hardly avoid tincturing the mind either with melancholy or superstition. "If a Christian may act in the several relations of life, must he seclude himself from all to become so? Surely the principles as well as the practice of Christianity are simple, and lead not to meditation only, but to action."

Finally, he dismissed out of hand the idea that they should not discuss the matter. Tomorrow, he said, was not too soon. "I am going into Kent and can take in Wimbledon on my way. Reflect, I beg you, that no principles are the worse for being discussed. . . ."

Wilberforce was much affected by this letter, signed "affectionately and unalterably yours," and next day they spent two hours together. Neither changed the other's view on fundamentals. Pitt, said Wilberforce years later, "tried to reason me out of my convictions, but soon found himself unable to combat their correctness, if Christianity were true." Wilberforce, however, was forced to admit that, so far as involvement in public life was concerned, "as far as I could conform to the world, with a perfect regard to my duty to God, myself and my fellows, I was bound to do it." "The two parted," comments Sir Reginald Coupland, "one fearing his country had lost a statesman, the other knowing that he had not lost a friend."

Within a few months Wilberforce's diary again began to record the familiar "Pitt's before the House and dined," and "Dined Pitt's and sat with him." Indeed, one who often saw them together at this time remarked that "they were exactly like brothers." Nevertheless there was a change in their relationship. Pitt could no longer tell Wilberforce to "tear the enemy in pieces" as in his note to York, and he turned increasingly to Henry Dundas, rather than Wilberforce, for counsel in House of Commons matters. Yet, as Sir Winston Churchill, surveying the whole period, noted in his *History of the English-Speaking Peoples*, Wilberforce was "the only person ever to enjoy Pitt's full confidence."

Wilberforce found the thought of seeing Newton much more disagreeable. To write to Pitt and other friends was one thing; to be seen by the world to be associating with so notorious a "Methodist" as Newton quite another. Partly because of fear of the religious "enthusiasm" which had led to Englishmen killing and persecuting each other in the preceding age, but mainly because of the way the more exacting standards pioneered by the Wesleys cut across the easy-going morals of the period, "Methodists"* were hated by the

---

*The term was used at the time for anyone who showed signs of living by the more exacting standards pioneered by the Wesleys. Neither Newton, Wilberforce nor John Wesley himself, who was still alive, ever left the Church of their birth. Wesley's spiritual revolution, which started from his "heart being strangely warmed" in 1728 had begun with the working classes and the outcasts and moved through the country like a flame. The degenerate English Church resisted it and it is said that no bishop's charge for forty years failed to condemn it. However, its spirit was now beginning to penetrate the upper echelons of society and, in Wilberforce's lifetime, would revive the Church which had rejected it.

Establishment with an intensity Wilberforce could only compare with that displayed towards the Jews in Scott's *Ivanhoe*. What sane politician, he asked himself, would subject himself to that?

The struggle in Wilberforce's heart is mirrored day by day in his journal. The thought to "go and converse with Mr. Newton" first came to him on November 30th, and again during the night. The December 2nd entry begins, "Resolved again about Mr. Newton . . . It can do no harm for this is a scandalous objection which keeps occurring to me, that if ever my sentiments change, I shall be ashamed of having done it . . . Kept debating." That day, he went so far as going to town to discover where Newton, now the vicar of St. Mary Woolnoth, lived. The entry for the following day starts: "Had a good deal of debate with myself about seeing Newton . . ." and resulted in his writing a letter and "delivering it" himself "to old Newton at his church" on December 4th. In the letter he admitted that his "ten thousand doubts" about seeing Newton were all founded on pride, yet he still tore his signature off the bottom and pressed Newton twice "to let no man living know of it" and to remember, in fixing any meeting, that an MP's face is very well known. So the meeting was fixed at Newton's house at Hoxton for December 7th. "When I came away," Wilberforce recorded, "I found my mind in a calm and tranquil state."

It was perhaps natural that the successful politician should find it hard to approach the man who typified the faith and affection he had known as a boy and then rejected to the point of ridicule. But the key reason for his hesitation was, of course, an unwillingness to identify himself with the most militant Christianity of the day. It proved to be a turning-point. By January 12th, Wilberforce was writing in his journal: "Expect to hear myself now universally given out as a Methodist: may God grant it may be said with truth."

Newton, like Pitt, counselled Wilberforce not to divide himself from his old friends. "The Lord has raised you up for the good of his church and for the good of the nation," he said. Both may therefore claim a share in retaining Wilberforce in public life. It was this decision which was to give Wilberforce that mature balance between the private and the public, between private holiness and care for the world, which is fundamental to Christianity, but yet is so often missed even by the most sincere.

Newton, the "old Africa blasphemer," as he called himself, stayed close to Wilberforce in the difficult months of adjustment after "the great change," which became all the more necessary because Isaac Milner, through helping Wilberforce, had been forced to reassess his own life and was in no condition spiritually to carry him forward. Newton was a man of confident faith and growing tenderness, as his hymns such as "Glorious Things of Thee Are Spoken" and "Amazing Grace," to name but two, show. He also reconciled Wilberforce to his Wimbledon aunt, Hannah, now living in Blackheath, and to her brother, John Thornton of Clapham, whose youngest son, Henry, was to become Wilberforce's closest colleague in the years ahead. He introduced him, too, to Hannah More, the wit and playwright, who had lived in her youth with Mr. and Mrs. Garrick and become one of the circle around Dr. Johnson and Sir Joshua Reynolds. Garrick had nicknamed her "Nine" (the embodiment of the nine muses) and Johnson judged her "the most powerful versificatrix in the language." Hannah had been experiencing a similar "change" to that of Wilberforce and they met at Bath the following year.

6

Seeking a Destiny

WILBERFORCE WAS NOW FACED with the momentous issue of how, in his new circumstances, he should conduct himself in public life. What amendments were needed in the way of life which had helped him to success? How would such changes affect his relationships with friends and constituents? And, above all, what should his new aims be if, as Newton said, he had been raised up for the good of his country? Such questions occupied his mind continuously during the next eighteen months. If 1785 was a year of decision, 1786 was a year of struggle and waiting. For a successful politician the implications were revolutionary.

Wilberforce began by clearing the decks. He resigned in one day from five fashionable clubs, gave up gambling and dancing and even, since it had become so "corrupt," going to the theatre. In terms of his political activities, meanwhile, he introduced two Bills in the Commons, one a further attempt at moderate Parliamentary reform and the other a rather fumbling humanitarian measure, but increasingly he felt that both his aims and motives needed radical revision. "The first years

I was in Parliament, I did nothing—nothing that is to any purpose," he wrote later. "My own distinction was my darling object."

While still welcome in the highest circles, he felt a certain awkwardness there, partly because he saw others and himself more clearly. His journal notes, "At the levee and then dined at Pitt's—sort of cabinet dinner—was often thinking that pompous Thurlow and elegant Carmarthen would soon appear in the same row with the poor fellow who waits behind the chairs." And again, "Dined at E's—rout afterwards—what extreme folly is all this! Yet much entertained." "Though the interest I took in my old friends was even greater than it had been before the change," he wrote, "yet, from obvious and natural causes, we were not likely to be such agreeable intimates to each other as heretofore."

He also feared that his new way of life might "excite disgust rather than cordiality" among his constituents. County Members were expected to progress through their constituencies, attending race meetings, balls and dinners, eating vast meals and drinking two or three bottles of wine at each occasion. Only the year before he had, in his sons' words "gone to the North on the prorogation of Parliament presenting himself at York as 'the joy' of the races" (he had owned a race horse at one point) and "spent his twenty-fifth birthday at the top wave and highest flow of those frivolous amusements, which had swallowed up so large a portion of his youth." What, he now asked Wyvill, would his robust constituents think of him cutting balls and missing race meetings? He was much relieved when Wyvill replied that, as the Government was popular and trade flourished, he did not feel a Member's progress necessary that year.

Meanwhile, his inner moral and spiritual struggle continued. He made rules for himself, and often did not keep them, but invariably went back to them. He made a serious examination of himself in the early mornings and on Sundays and kept lists of his "chief besetting sins" and "the chief Christian graces which I want to cultivate." Often his battles were to get to bed by eleven "whenever possible" and up at six, or to avoid "temptations of the table," which, however trivial in themselves, "disqualify me for every useful purpose in life, waste my time, impair my health, fill my mind with resistance before and self-condemnation afterwards." He was particularly mortified when he saw Pitt and his cousin, Bob Smith, practising restraint and only eating and drinking to excess "at seasons of jollity, whereas I do it merely from brutal sensuality of animal satisfaction."

At about this time, he made a pact with Milner to pay a forfeit, presumably to charity, for lapses pointed out by the other. It had to be abandoned because the guineas flowed too copiously from Wilberforce to Milner, since the gargantuan Milner cheerfully ignored in himself the "sins of the table" on which Wilberforce was so sensitive.

In these early days, Wilberforce's drastic amendment of life might seem a rather grim affair. By mid-1786, however, he had recovered much of the gaiety which delighted his friends. If "gravity" should be the business of life, "gaiety," he told his sister, should be its relaxation. "I will give it a more worthy epithet than gay," he added. "Let me call it serenity, tranquility, composure which can not be destroyed." And this seems to have made its mark when he visited his family in Scarborough. His mother, who had been thoroughly alarmed by reports of his return to "Methodism," was pleasantly surprised by his cheerfulness and the disappearance of his quick temper. "If this is madness," said her friend, Mrs. Sykes, "I hope he will bite us all." The change was the more startling because the sea and the heat and the dust had so disordered his eyes that he had seldom known them so bad. His sister and some of the Smith cousins quickly caught his faith, but their brother, Bob Smith (later Lord Carrington) remarked: "He knows he can not convert me."

Others, elsewhere, were also noticing the change. Edward Eliot, who had married Pitt's favourite sister, Harriot, had been a member of Goosetrees where he was nicknamed "Sir Bull," probably because of his premarital sexual adventures. Harriot died in childbirth in September 1786 and both Eliot and Pitt were thrown into a "state of dreadful agitation." Wilberforce's friendship was Eliot's main support in the months that followed. He grew to share Wilberforce's faith, and the two frequently opened their hearts to each other. Eliot was Member for Liskeard and both knew the difficulties of walking with God in the day-to-day pressures of politics. "Pray for me, my dear friend, as I do for you," Wilberforce wrote to him. "We can render each other no more effectual service." "I was little better than an infidel, but it pleased God to call me to a better mind," was Eliot's assessment.

Henry Thornton, the youngest son of Wilberforce's Clapham uncle, John, soon followed. He had been repelled, in youth, by the hypocrisy he perceived in some of his father's pious business associates, but he found Wilber, as most of Wilberforce's relatives and friends called him, an entirely different proposition. "My education was narrow," Thornton wrote in later life, "and his enlarged mind, his affectionate and understanding manners and his very superior piety were exactly calculated to supply what was wanting to my improvement and my establishment in the right course."

That Henry's former "disgust" with hypocrisy was genuine is illustrated by the fact that he had turned down the chance to succeed Wilberforce as Member for Hull because he could not agree to give bribes. The following year he won a tough election in Southwark without bribery. The cousins were to prove exactly complementary to each other, for where "Wilber" was intuitive, Henry was all quiet deliberation. He was to become Wilberforce's closest colleague.

Others who became disciples of Wilberforce at about this time included Matthew Montague MP and Lord Muncaster. Henry Bankes, another Goosetrees friend and MP for Dorset, also became increasingly identified with him, whether because of affection or a shared faith is not clear, since his papers have been lost. Bob Smith never was "converted," although Wilberforce made another attempt as late as 1829 at Carrington's home, Wykeham Abbey, but he was a sympathetic ally and, as he said, "they always met in kindness."

One further fruit of Wilberforce's own change was a new intellectual rigour. He set himself to redeem the idle years at Cambridge, reading Montesquieu, Blackstone, Adam Smith, Locke and Pope and, with particular delight, Samuel Johnson. From this time until his marriage, twenty years later, he spent two months every summer in such study. Usually he settled down in the country house of one of his friends such as Gisborne, who was now both squire and parson at Yoxall Lodge in Staffordshire. Later, the topic under examination would often be evidence for some Parliamentary battle and the reading would go on nine hours a day. In this year of waiting it was, above all, the Bible which became his favourite book. As he travelled, too, he carried a notebook in which he entered information from his innumerable conversations. "I should ask for facts not opinions," he always advised young researchers.

Through all this year of 1786, Wilberforce was still looking for the distinctive part he was meant to play in public life. As he watched London society with new eyes, he was clear that he must fight to bring a new moral tone to the leadership of Britain. But was there any particular cause in which he should be engaged? The answer came to him, most unexpectedly, through his feckless, but amusing, college friend, Gerard Edwards.

Gerard's father-in-law was Captain Sir Charles Middleton, the Comptroller of the Navy and, at the time of Wilberforce's conversion, one of only two publicly known Evangelicals in the House of Commons. Lady Middleton, a painter and intellectual with similar friends to Hannah More, had been converted while a girl through George Whitefield. The Middletons lived at Teston and round them had gathered a group of people dedicated to the abolition of the Slave Trade.

This was due largely to an incident which had befallen Sir Charles when he was in the West Indies in command of HMS *Arundel*. There, in November 1759, he had recaptured the

Bristol slave ship, *Swift*, from the French and sent his surgeon, James Ramsay, on board to investigate. Plague was raging and neither he nor Ramsay ever forgot what they saw. Ramsay's convictions were heightened when he became Rector and medical supervisor of the plantations in St. Kitt's, and now, as Vicar of Teston, he had written two books, one an indictment of slavery itself and the second of the Slave Trade. A tremendous war of words ensued and Teston became a centre of information and agitation against the Trade. It was there in 1786 that Bishop Porteous of Chester, himself a Virginian by birth, called a conference on the subject and it was to Teston two months later, that Thomas Clarkson, who had just published his Cambridge prize essay, *Slavery and Commerce in the Human Species*, came almost by accident. At dinner there, he renewed the vow, already made privately, to devote his whole time to fighting the Trade. He was the first to do so and his intrepid research, often at the risk of his life, provided much of the evidence which was to sustain the Abolitionist fight.

Public opinion against the Slave Trade, then, was rising from many sides by the autumn of 1786; but it was clear to Lady Middleton that a trade so important to Britain could not be suppressed without Parliamentary action. Sir Charles, who was engaged in a radical reform of the Navy, was unwilling to take on a task which even Burke had considered beyond his powers. However, Lady Middleton was insistent and forced her husband, over breakfast one morning, to go through a list of possible Parliamentary sponsors. They lighted on Gerard's friend Wilberforce, who soon received a letter from Sir Charles asking him to raise the matter in the House. Wilberforce replied that he felt unequal to the task, but "could not possibly decline." He felt "the great importance of the subject."

Opinions differ whether this was Wilberforce's first serious consideration of the matter, but it is certainly from this time that he became deeply involved. Clarkson visited him regularly that winter at 4 Palace Yard, the house opposite the entrance of the House of Lords, which he bought that year to replace his Wimbledon villa. These meetings with Clarkson were crucial, for now Wilberforce began to study the question deeply, and, in the spring, he held a series of dinners at his new home to consider Parliamentary action.

The final stimulus came from Pitt himself. On May 12th, 1787, Pitt, his cousin Grenville and Wilberforce, all three now men of twenty-seven, were lolling beneath an oak overlooking the Vale of Keston. "Wilberforce," said Pitt, "why don't you give notice of a motion on the subject of the Slave Trade?" In later years, Wilberforce always recalled that scene when asked how he entered the battle for Abolition.

Meanwhile, he was still intensely concerned in his morning hours with the need of a moral rebirth in the country. On October 28th he summed up his growing commitment in his journal. "God Almighty," he wrote, "has set before me two great objects: the suppression of the slave trade and the reformation of manners." The two were, of course, intimately related. On the one hand, it would take a profound moral reformation in leaders and people to obtain the suppression of so cherished a trade; on the other, only an unselfish battle like the abolition of the Trade would demonstrate to God and the world that such a moral reformation was genuine. Wilberforce decided to wage both campaigns simultaneously and he set both under way in 1787.

7

"The Execrable Villainy"

THE CAMPAIGN TO SUPPRESS the Slave Trade was to occupy twenty years of unremitting toil. During this period, Wilberforce was to become one of the most hated men in England—and one of the most beloved. In the world outside, he became one of the best known of all his countrymen and the one who did most to create a new idea of England as a country capable of altruism. Few foreigners had entertained such a possibility before, but the way in which Wilberforce spent his time and talents on the good of mankind as a whole made a deep impression. A strain of altruism was then introduced into the British political tradition which has never quite faded.

In 1787, as Wilberforce and his friends consulted with the Quakers' Abolition Committee on how best to initiate Parliamentary action, three main themes occupied their minds. These were the wrongs done to the African continent, the horrors of the Slave Trade and the evils of slavery itself. The question was which of these intermingled evils to attack first.

From the beginning, their ultimate aim was to end slavery

itself and make what reparation was possible to the continent of Africa, but Wilberforce knew that immediate emancipation was politically impractical. So he and his friends decided that their first aim must be to stop the supply of slaves, thus eliminating the cruelties of the Trade and, it was hoped, forcing planters to treat their present slaves better because they would be irreplaceable. He urged everyone to avoid even mentioning the word "emancipation" at this stage.

After his talk with Pitt and Grenville, Wilberforce was confident that the Trade itself could be abolished quickly. At first, he hoped that much could be achieved by diplomatic agreement with the French, but this proved impossible. So, soon after Christmas 1787, he gave notice that he would introduce a motion early in the new session to abolish the Slave Trade. Fox rose from the Opposition front bench and promised his support and other leaders were encouraging. Wilberforce was extremely optimistic. "As to our probability of success," he wrote, "I entertain no doubt of it." His confidence was based on "the evident, the glaring justice of the proposition itself; Mr. Pitt's support and the disposition of the House."

Wilberforce's optimism was not shared by John Wesley, now in his 84th year and wise in the reactions of his countrymen when confronted by costly moral principle. He warned Granville Sharp to expect "all the opposition which can be made by men who are not encumbered by either Honour, Conscience or Humanity . . . who will rush on through every possible means, to secure their great Goddess, interest." Neither money nor "a thousand arguments" would be spared "in raising every possible objection against you."

A thousand arguments were indeed deployed, for the opposition was widespread and passionate. The great sailor, Admiral Lord Rodney, declared that he had never known a slave ill-treated during his time in the West Indies, while Lord Heathfield, the defender of Gibraltar, announced that a slave on the way to the Indies had twice as much cubic air space as a British soldier in a regulation tent. A group of admirals went further. It was, they said, the happiest day of an African's life when he was shipped away from the barbarities of his home land.

The mass of Members simply feared change. They were told, and believed, that sacred rights, property and liberties were threatened, both at home and in the colonies. This was the view of Admiral Lord Nelson, the nation's greatest hero. He wrote from his flagship, *Victory*: "I was bred in the good old school and taught to appreciate the value of our West Indian possessions, and neither in the field nor in the Senate shall their just rights be infringed, while I have an arm to fight in their defence or a tongue to launch my voice against the damnable doctrine of Wilberforce and his hypocritical allies."

Wilberforce's opponents made every effort to keep humanity out of the argument. The *Zong* case had established that slaves were simply chattels, and that a ship's captain had the unquestionable right at law to dump as many overboard as he wished "without any suggestion of cruelty or surmise of impropriety." "Humanity," the Earl of Abingdon was to declare in the debate, "is a private feeling and not a public principle to act upon." Admiral Lord St. Vincent added that: "The whole of society would go to pieces if the wedge of abstract right were once entered into any part of it."

Wilberforce, working feverishly on the evidence for his first motion, was only partly aware of the feeling against him. Pitt saw more clearly. He knew that the Royal Family and most of his Cabinet, Secretary of State Sydney, and Chancellor, Thurlow, for example, were firmly opposed to Abolition. Convinced that only facts could change opinion, he therefore peremptorily ordered the Trade and Plantations Committee of the Privy Council to investigate the Slave Trade and Britain's commercial relations with Africa generally.

At this apparently critical moment Wilberforce fell ill. He continued his preparations from his bed at Palace Yard, but by mid-February exhaustion and fever, with loss of sleep and appetite, had overcome him. Lord Muncaster and Matthew Montague constituted themselves his principal nurses; Mrs.

Wilberforce and Sally were sent for and two eminent doctors, James Pitcairn and Richard Warren, were called in. "That little fellow with calico guts can not possibly last a twelve month," said Warren, while a conference of doctors declared that he had "not the stamina to last a fortnight." The Fitzwilliam interest in Yorkshire, hearing that Wilberforce was dying, made plans to recapture the seat.

By mid-March, however, the crisis was passed by means of the use of opium, a common remedy in those days for what seems to have been a case of ulcerated colitis. In April the patient left for Bath to take the waters. Before leaving, he asked Pitt to move the Slave Trade resolution in his place. Pitt, throwing caution, party difficulties and royal coldness to the winds, "with a warmth of principle and friendship that have made me love him better than ever before" promised so to do. It was therefore the Prime Minister who, on April 7th, 1788, moved that the House investigate the Trade. His motion was not as definite as Wilberforce may have wished and his speech was one of studied neutrality, but there was now no doubt where Pitt's sympathies lay. A few months later, when the Lords threatened to throw out a minor Commons measure requiring more space to be provided for slaves on board ships, the Prime Minister let it be known that he and any Lords who voted against it could not remain in the same Cabinet.

Wilberforce was not fit enough to return to the Commons until November, when he hastened back to support Pitt in the crisis following the King's first illness. George III had gone out of his mind, in what we now know to have been a case of hereditary porphyria, and the Opposition were demanding a Regency by their patron the Prince of Wales as of right, without debate. Pitt was determined that, if a Regent proved necessary, he must be appointed under conditions decided by Parliament. Many months were absorbed with this question and it was not until May 1789 that Wilberforce was able to put Abolition flatly before the Commons. He prepared his speech at Teston with what Hannah More called the "Anti-Slave

Junta," which had just been reinforced by James Stephen,* a brilliant lawyer newly returned from the West Indies. Gisborne, who was in the country, wrote to Wilberforce cheerfully: "I shall expect to read of your being carbanadoed by West Indian planters, barbecued by African merchants and eaten by Guinea captains, but do not be daunted, for—I will write your epitaph!"

On the morning of the debate Wilberforce arrived in London feeling unwell, but nonetheless spoke for three and a half hours extemporaneously, using only some headings which are still preserved in the Bodleian Library in Oxford University. He now realized that most of his audience agreed in their hearts about the inhumanity of the Trade, but were extremely cautious of damaging an essential national interest. There was also the West Indian lobby of some sixty Members to consider. He was therefore careful to speak with the utmost courtesy and moderation. Burke, later that evening, judged his speech "the equal of anything he had heard of in modern oratory and perhaps not excelled by anything to be met with in Demosthenes."

Wilberforce began by urging Members to approach the question without passion, to give a cool and impartial verdict: "I mean not to accuse anyone," he said, "but to take the shame upon myself, in common indeed with the whole Parliament of Britain, for having suffered this horrid trade to be carried on under their authority. We are all guilty—we ought all to plead guilty, and not to exculpate ourselves by throwing the blame on others."

For his part, he went on, he was so convinced of the

*Stephen practised at the West Indies bar, but never owned a slave. Early in his stay in St. Christopher he witnessed a farcical trial of two negroes who were sentenced to be burnt to death. He became the most passionate of all the Abolitionists. "I would rather be on friendly terms with a man who had strangled my infant son than support an Administration slack in the suppression of the slave trade." In 1789 he was a great help in drafting Wilberforce's case, and when in 1794 he returned permanently to England he quickly made his name at the Admiralty Bar. He became one of Wilberforce's closest friends and in 1800 married his sister, Sarah.

mischiefs inseparable from the Trade that he needed no
further evidence. But facts were now before the House, and he
took Members through the Privy Council evidence of the effect
of the Trade on Africa and of the horrors of the Middle
Passage. In almost his only resort to sarcasm, he contrasted the
lyrical description of the slaves' "pleasure cruise," as evi-
denced by their dancing on deck, to the Indies, as described by
a Mr. Norris of Liverpool, with the fearful truth.

Turning to the West Indies, he courteously conceded that
absentee planters sent out admirable orders and that manag-
ers did not intend to be cruel. They just looked on slaves as a
different species, for which they could feel no sympathy. He
pointed out that stopping the supply of slaves would oblige
planters to treat existing slaves better, and that stronger,
healthier slaves would work harder and procreate more, thus
building up a better labour force without the expense of new
purchases. Far from being ruined, the sugar islands would
prosper.

He dealt with the arguments of his opponents: that
Liverpool would be ruined, that the French would take over
the Trade, that the supply of trained sailors, essential for the
navy, would decrease. "More sailors die in one year in the
Slave Trade," he said, using Clarkson's brief, "than die in two
years in all the other trades put together." It was the grave, not
the nursery, of seamen.

He had considered regulation and other palliatives, but
was convinced that the Trade's wickedness was so enormous
and immediate that only total Abolition would cure the evil. He
concluded:

> I trust . . . I have proved that, upon every ground, total abo-
> lition ought to take place. I have urged many things which
> are not my own leading motives for proposing it, since I have
> wished to show every description of gentlemen, and particu-
> larly the West India planters, who deserve every attention,
> that the abolition is politic upon their own principles. Policy,
> however, Sir, is not my principle, and I am not ashamed to

say it. There is a principle above everything that is politic,
and when I reflect on the command which says: "Thou shalt
do no murder," believing its authority to be divine, how can
I dare to set up any reasonings of my own against it? . . .

Sir, the nature and all the circumstances of this Trade are
now laid open to us. We can no longer plead ignorance. We
cannot evade it. We may spurn it. We may kick it out of the
way. But we cannot turn aside so as to avoid seeing it. For it
is brought now so directly before our eyes that this House
must decide and must justify to all the world and to its own
conscience, the rectitude of the grounds of its decision . . .
Let not Parliament be the only body that is insensible to the
principles of natural justice. Let us make reparation to Africa,
as far as we can, by establishing trade upon true commercial
principles, and we shall soon find the rectitude of our conduct rewarded by the benefits of a regular and growing commerce.

Burke, Pitt and Fox followed, wholehearted in their
support, but much of the House was uneasy, swayed by
Wilberforce's facts, yet worried that Abolition might bring
economic disaster. It was upon this argument that his opponents, the Member for Liverpool and sundry gentlemen with
sugar interests, at first relied. When the debate was resumed
nine days later, however, they had thought of a new tactic.
Lord Maitland argued that the House would surrender its
historic rights if it accepted evidence given before the Privy
Council and did not insist on its being presented at the Bar to
the House itself. The House seized upon this argument and
constituted itself a committee to hear evidence on nine
particular days during the summer. It then promptly adjourned
the matter until the next session. Members could not justly
plead ignorance, but a way of escape had been provided.

The opponents of Abolition favoured a Committee of the
whole House. They believed that, since the evidence against
Abolition was to be given first, boredom among Members at
large would prevent too much contrary evidence from being

received. Wilberforce countered by proposing a Select Committee, but one which any Member would have the right to attend, and this, after a struggle, was agreed. When the evidence on behalf of the Trade was concluded in April 1790, however, its supporters tried to get a snap decision before evidence against it could be heard. Wilberforce heard of this, mobilized his forces and won the right to continue.

As the battle went on, Wilberforce's home in Palace Yard became more and more chaotic. "During the sitting of Parliament," he wrote a friend, "my house is a mere hotel." The Prime Minister and his friends dined there so often that Wilberforce was rumoured to receive a pension for feeding them. The Slave Committee dined there once a week and Clarkson and the other researchers—Wilberforce's "white negroes" Pitt called them—did much of their work there. His ante-room was full from early morning; the first arrivals usually being invited in to breakfast. The variety was amazing: Yorkshire constituents, missionaries, Africans, petitioners for and receivers of charity, as well as politicians or even an eminent statesman, forgotten in the confusion. Hannah More described it as a "Noah's ark, full of beasts clean and unclean." Originally it was lined with books of a size which Wilberforce could slip into his pocket to read while walking, but these also fitted into other peoples' pockets, and so many disappeared that they had to be replaced by less portable volumes.

As spring of 1790 passed into summer, witnesses came and went in Committee, with Wilberforce doggedly in attendance. In early June the process was interrupted by a General Election and Wilberforce wondered whether his cause and the many changes he had made in his way of living would prevent his re-election. The Fitzwilliam interest had high hopes, but a canvass showed such overwhelming support for Wilberforce and Duncombe that they were again returned without a poll.

After the election, Wilberforce went on a tour of Wales with Thomas Babington, another St. John's contemporary now in Parliament. Unlike Gisborne, he had been repelled by

Wilberforce's Cambridge frivolity, but had since become a close friend. After the Welsh tour, the two of them settled into Gisborne's country house to study the enormous volume of evidence on the Trade presented before the Privy Council and the 1,400 pages of evidence already delivered to the House of Commons. They worked nine or ten hours a day, seldom went out and often did not stop for meals. Later, Wilberforce moved to John Thornton's house at Clapham for the same purpose. "Sunday as a working day—did not go to Church—Slave Trade," for him the ultimate sacrifice, began to appear regularly in his diary.

The new Parliament gathered, and Wilberforce wanted to continue the evidence at once, but the Committee's sittings were not resumed till February 1791. There were, however, signs that Abolitionists were beginning to gain support in the country. The print of Clarkson's model of the slave ship *Brookes*, showing how 450 slaves were packed in like sardines for the Middle Passage, had been widely circulated; Cowper's poem *The Negro's Complaint* gained popularity; and Josiah Wedgwood, the distinguished potter, had produced a cameo of a negro in chains begging for compassion, inscribed "Am I not a Man and a Brother?" The Abolitionists were also winning the pamphlet war, and it was clear that the Trade's evidence was coming largely from financially interested parties.

But there were other less favourable developments. The revolution in France was gathering momentum, and a rising of slaves had taken place in St. Dominique. An Irish Member attributed the rising to the slaves' belief that the Governor had the authority of the British Parliament and of *Massa King Wilberforce* to pay them and restrict their work to three days a week. The planters regarded this as a trump card. "Surely," wrote the slave owner's agent in Antigua, "the Enthusiastic rage of Mr. Wilberforce and his friends can not prevail in a matter of such consequence to the Colonies and the Mother Country." But Fuller, the Jamaica agent in London, was not so sanguine. "It is necessary to watch him," he replied, "as he is blessed with a very sufficient quantity of that Enthusiastic spirit which is so far from yielding that it grows more vigorous with blows."

John Wesley, in what was probably the last letter he ever wrote, put the fight in perspective. He wrote to Wilberforce on February 24th:

> My dear sir,
> Unless the Divine Power has raised you up to be an *Athanasius contra mundum* I see not how you can go through with your glorious enterprise in opposing that execrable villainy which is the scandal of religion, of England and of human nature. Unless God has raised you up for this very thing, you will be worn out by the opposition of men and devils; but if God is with you, who can be against you? Are all of them stronger than God? Oh, be not weary in well-doing. Go on, in the name of God and in the power of His might, till even American slavery, the vilest that ever saw the sun, shall vanish away before it . . . That he who has guided you from your youth up, may continue to strengthen you in this and in all things, is the prayer of
> Dear Sir, your affectionate servant,
> John Wesley

So, on April 18th, 1791, Wilberforce once again moved the House for the Abolition of the Trade. He spoke for four hours, and the debate proceeded very much as before. Burke, Pitt and Fox again backed Wilberforce, with Fox, by general consent, making the most effective speech. A spokesman of the Trade put their case bluntly. It was not an amiable traffic, but neither was that of a butcher, yet a mutton chop was a good thing. Others pretended that only criminals, including adulterers, were taken from Africa as slaves. "Was adultery, then, a crime we needed to go to Africa to punish?" asked Fox, peering round the House. "Was this the way we took to establish the purity of our national character? . . . It was a most extraordinary pilgrimage for a most extraordinary purpose." His speech, magnificent in its range and logic, made a deep

impression and when he sat down, Stanley, Lord Derby's son
and a prominent Lancashire Member, announced that he had
come to the House to vote against Abolition but was now
convinced that total Abolition was the only course. Dudley
Ryder, whose dress hat Pitt had once sown in Wilberforce's
Wimbledon flower beds, also changed sides. Yet the motion
was still lost by 88 to 163.

One of Wilberforce's opponents in the debate described it
as a battle between giants and pygmies. The giants won the
argument, but the pygmies were too many for them. The sixty
Members of the West Indian lobby provided a nucleus around
which the cautious and the callous gathered. Dread of the
influence of the French Revolution in Britain, which was to
turn Pitt's administration from one sympathetic to reform into
one of safety-first repression, was already having its effect,
although that fear was not to reach its peak until 1793. Fear
that the French might take over the Trade and a feeling that
Abolition was not an urgent matter were enough to ensure this
present defeat. Wilberforce and his friends, on the other hand,
felt passionately that every day during which it was allowed to
continue meant untold agony for thousands.

The country, meanwhile, was rallying to Wilberforce. In
the months after the 1791 defeat, 517 petitions for Abolition
flowed in to Westminster with only four against. Even Liverpool abstained. In an unreformed Parliament, however, these
petitions had only a marginal effect; but Wilberforce had no
thought of withdrawing. In his opening speech in 1791 he had
said that he had attached his happiness to the slaves' cause
and would never relinquish it. After defeat, he vowed that he
would raise the issue every year until the Trade was utterly
abolished. This he proceeded to do.

In 1792 he was pressed on all sides to defer his motion
because of the slaves' revolt in St. Dominique in 1791.
"People here are all panic stricken with those transactions in
St. Dominique," he wrote, "and the apprehension of the like
in Jamaica," where, incidentally, slaves outnumbered whites
by 16 to one. Wilberforce nevertheless insisted on moving for

Abolition. Again the giants thundered, Pitt making one of the greatest speeches of his life. The Abolitionists were carrying the day, until Henry Dundas eased the conscience of the House by suggesting that the word "gradual" be inserted before "abolition" in Wilberforce's motion. The House gratefully carried this amended motion by 230 to 85. Thus the Trade was for the first time officially condemned by the House and Wilberforce was universally congratulated. He himself was nonetheless bitterly disappointed. Dundas went on to suggest 1800 as a target date for Abolition and the House finally settled on 1796; but the measure sank into the quicksands of the House of Lords.

After this debate, the Abolition issue was never quite the same. The House had overwhelmingly agreed that Abolition in some form was necessary, but Dundas had cooled off the lukewarm abolitionists and other "moderate men" by his specious promise that justice would be done if only they would be patient. By admitting that the Trade was abhorrent and unnecessary, he deprived Wilberforce of his strongest arguments and left his opponents only needing to show, year after year, that the times were inconvenient. As war with France developed, such arguments gained in force.

Soon after the debate, Wilberforce's life was twice threatened by West Indian sea captains. One began waylaying him in the street and his friends pressed him to accept an armed bodyguard. "I can't say I apprehend much," he wrote to Muncaster, "as I really believe that if he were to commit any act of violence it would be beneficial rather than injurious to the cause." He was more concerned when the Revolutionary French Convention made him an honourary Citizen of France, along with his own and Parliament's *bete noir*, Thomas Paine. Jeremy Bentham,* who was similarly honoured, could take this more lightly. "Looking through the list," he wrote to

---

*Jeremy Bentham, the most famous political philosopher of the day, was the founder of Utilitarianism.

Wilberforce, "I observe 6 British: and among these 6, none but yourself and your humble servant that are not *reputed* Republicans, unless it be your journeyman labourer in the Vineyards of the Slave Trade, Mr. Clarkson, of whose sentiments in constitutional matters I am not apprised." Clarkson, like Fox, had welcomed the French Revolution with enthusiasm, and this, together with Wilberforce's acceptance of the "doubtful honour" provided welcome ammunition to the Slave interest in the years ahead.

8

Struggle and Triumph

WAR WITH FRANCE CAME in February 1793. Wilberforce had neither welcomed the Revolution like Paine nor opposed it root and branch like Burke. Indeed he thought Burke such a menace to peace that he exclaimed, "O that I could transport him to some fertile island in the Great South Sea." He was no pacifist, but he feared that war would delay moderate electoral reform, set back his "reformation of manners," though in fact it did just the opposite, and relegate the abolition of the Slave Trade into a measure of minor importance. So he sought to restrain Pitt until the last, urging various schemes for containing France while avoiding war. He did not succeed.

The war's effect upon the Slave issue was swiftly confirmed. When Wilberforce reintroduced the successful motion for "Gradual Abolition," he was defeated by eight votes in a thin House and even more decisively in the Lords. The gains of the previous year had been swept away.

So he decided to try a new tactic. In March 1793 he sought leave to bring forward a Bill (The Foreign Slave Bill) to prohibit the carrying of slaves to foreign territories in British ships and won permission by seven votes in a House of only 79. When, nine days later, he moved the Bill, he lost by two votes in an almost empty House.

In 1794, he again succeeded in passing the Foreign Slave Bill by majorities of 23 and 18 in the Commons. For the first time Henry Dundas, the new Secretary of State for War and the Colonies, came out uncompromisingly against him, and Wilberforce's elation faded when the Foreign Secretary decided not to bring the Bill forward in the Lords where, in Fuller's phrase, it went "fast asleep."

Two years later, he had the highest hopes of success when, by astute tactics, he won a second reading for a Bill advocating full Abolition. This, of course, was the year when, according to Dundas' "gradual" motion, Abolition should have been granted, and a count of heads encouraged Wilberforce to believe that he would also carry the Third Reading on the night of March 15th. It was, however, the first night of a new Italian opera, *The Two Hunchbacks*, at Covent Garden and when the motion was lost by 70 to 74, it became clear that at least half a dozen of those pledged to vote for him had preferred music to conscience. Some said that Dundas, who was in his place to vote against the motion, had conveniently supplied them with tickets. Wilberforce noted in his diary, "This week I have occasionally felt a sinful anger about the slave-carrying Bill and the scandalous neglect of its friends," but nine years later when there was another failure at the same hurdle and the Clerk of the Commons kindly remarked that, with his experience of life, Wilberforce really should not expect to pass such a measure, he replied: "I do expect to carry it; and what is more, I feel assured that I shall carry it speedily." This was in 1805, when his motion was lost by 70 to 77.

Indeed, the years between had been strewn with small defeats, 74 to 82 in 1797, 83 to 87 in 1798 and 54 to 84 in 1799, when George III intervened directly in the battle. In 1800 Wilberforce lost the chance to introduce the matter when it seemed that the planters, moved by economic changes, might negotiate. In 1804, when he actually won the day in the

House of Commons by 124 to 49, he was again frustrated in
the Lords, when four Royal Dukes attended to vote him down.

Through all these years, Wilberforce's expectancy was
kept high and his determination firm by what Pollock calls "the
steel spring" within him. He had explained its origin as far back
as 1793.

> In the case of every question of political expediency [he
> wrote in a private letter] there appears to me room for con-
> sideration of times and seasons—at one period, under one
> set of circumstances it may be proper to push, at another,
> under another set of circumstances, to withhold our efforts.
> But in the present instance where the actual commission of
> guilt is in question, a man who fears God is not at liberty. To
> you I will say a strong thing which the motive I have sug-
> gested will both explain and justify. If I thought that the im-
> mediate Abolition of the Slave Trade would cause an insur-
> rection in our islands, I should not for an instant remit my
> most serious endeavours. Be persuaded then, I shall still even
> less make this grand cause the sport of caprice, or sacrifice it
> to motives of political convenience or personal feeling.

When, in 1805, he made his confident reply to the Clerk
of the Commons, he was nearer to success than most men
dreamed. It was a year crowded with events: the victory of
Trafalgar and the death of Nelson; Napoleon's victory at
Austerlitz and the abandonment of his plan to invade Britain;
and, closest of all to Wilberforce's heart, the beginning of Pitt's
fatal illness. Pitt died in January 1806 and, paradoxically, his
death accelerated the coming of Abolition. For of late Pitt's
eagerness had cooled under the pressures of ill-health and
conflicting interests. In 1804 he had even spoken against one
of Wilberforce's measures.

Pitt was succeeded by his cousin, Lord Grenville, the third
of the young men who had discussed Abolition under the oak
at Keston eighteen years before. Fox joined his "Ministry of
All-the-Talents"; "quite rampant," noted an astonished Wil-

berforce, "and playful as he was twenty-two years ago. He talked as if we might certainly carry our question in the House of Commons but should certainly lose it in the House of Lords."

At this point Wilberforce's brother-in-law, James Stephen, had an idea which was to lead straight to victory. The previous September, and after much pressure from Wilberforce, Pitt had issued an Order in Council forbidding the importation of slaves into Dutch Guinea, which the British had captured. It was an order which pleased British planters since they assumed the colony would be returned to Holland after the war. Orders in Council frequently had to be consolidated into a Bill. So Stephen suggested that they persuade the Government to bring in a Bill confirming the Guinea Order and that they quietly tack onto it the prohibitions of Wilberforce's oft-defeated Foreign Slave Bill, forbidding British ships to carry slaves to any foreign territories. Being a Bill which derived from an Order in Council, it would have to be a Government measure and most supporters of the Ministry would vote for it as a war measure. The beauty of the scheme was not only that anti-Abolition members of the Cabinet could be expected to vote for it, but that British planters, whom the war had put at a disadvantage to their neutral and enemy rivals,* would favour it.

Wilberforce was actually on his way across Palace Yard to give notice of a motion for general Abolition when Stephen met him and explained his revolutionary plan. Wilberforce

---

*For example, British ships were landing slaves in neutral Dutch islands for transhipment to enemy territories, thus helping the enemy's economy. Also, enemy colonies were directly benefiting from the war. Neutral trade with these colonies did not bear the cost of the convoy system which British shipping had to pay. So American ships could take enemy sugar to Napoleon's Europe while British planters could not find a market for their inevitably more expensive sugar. Stephen had argued in *The War in Disguise* the year before that a belligerent had the right to search neutral ships and condemn cargoes bound for enemy ports, and the country had accepted his arguments. All this would mean the weakening of the British planters' rivals in the West Indies and reduce their need of extra slave labour.

agreed immediately, seeing that his own motion must be delayed until the Government measure was passed. Where Pitt would have dallied, Grenville and Fox acted at once and the tactic worked.

The Government's new Bill prohibited the importation of slaves in British ships into colonies of any foreign State or into those colonies annexed by Britain during the war. It also forbade the outfitting of foreign slave ships in British ports. The Duke of Clarence (the future William IV) once more spoke against the Bill, but Wilberforce's friend, the Duke of Gloucester, followed his royal cousin in a maiden speech condemning "a shocking traffic in human blood" and Fox was able, for the first time, to secure the neutrality of the Prince of Wales.

Fox and Grenville intended from the first that this Bill should be followed by another abolishing the entire Trade, the passing of which, said Fox, "would bestow more true glory upon this Administration and more honour upon our country than any other transaction on which we could be engaged." Fox took the first step on 10th June 1806, by moving a resolution which was passed by both Houses. "If it please God to spare the health of Fox," Wilberforce commented, "I hope we shall see next year a termination of our labours."

In fact Fox was dying of dropsy, but by now the tide for Abolition was flowing too strongly to be dammed. It was decided to start the final push where the measure had always been obstructed—in the Lords. So, on January 2nd 1807, "A Bill for the Abolition of the Slave Trade" was read there on the Prime Minister's motion. The first clause provided that, after May 1st, the African Slave Trade and "all manner of dealing and Trading in the purchase of slaves or their transport from Africa to the West Indies or any other territory is utterly abolished, prohibited and declared to be unlawful." The second declared that any British ship employed in the Trade thereafter should be forfeit to the Crown. Further clauses dealt with a number of lesser points.

Clarence and his diehard allies in the Lords delayed matters for a month, but when Grenville opened the debate

with a tribute to Wilberforce, ten speakers supported him and
only seven opposed. The reading was carried by a majority of
64. "Several peers," Wilberforce remarked, "now speak with
quite new civility . . . How striking to observe Pitt and Fox both
dead before Abolition effected, and now Lord Grenville,
without any particular defence from Court, carries it so
triumphantly." Truth to tell, Wilberforce had never liked
Grenville and now, as with Fox, he saw his mistake.

In the Commons the Foreign Secretary, Lord Howick
(later the Earl Grey of the Reform Bill), introduced the Bill for
Abolition, which was now for the first time a Government
measure there. Only one or two Members spoke against it.
The high point was reached when the Attorney-General, Sir
Samuel Romilly, wound up with a famous peroration:

> When I look [he said] to the man at the head of the French
> monarchy, surrounded as he is with all the pomp of power
> and all the price of victory, distributing kingdoms to his family
> and principalities to his followers, seeming when he sits upon
> his throne to have reached the summit of human ambition
> and the pinnacle of earthly happiness—and when I follow
> that man into his closet or to his bed, and consider the pangs
> with which his solitude must be tortured and his repose ban-
> ished, by the recollection of the blood he has spilled and the
> oppressions he has committed—and when I compare with
> those pangs of remorse the feelings which must accompany
> my honourable friend from this House to his home, after the
> vote of this night shall have confirmed the object of his hu-
> mane and unceasing labours; when he retires into the bosom
> of his happy and delighted family, when he lays himself
> down on his bed, reflecting on the innumerable voices that
> will be raised in every quarter of the world to bless him, how
> much more pure and perfect felicity must he enjoy, in the
> consciousness of having preserved so many millions of his
> fellow-creatures—than . . .

Before Romilly could finish, the storm of cheering broke

out, round after round. Wilberforce was scarcely aware of it. When Romilly spoke of his welcome home, his feelings overcame him and he sat, head in hands, the tears streaming down his face. Soon afterwards the House divided; the second reading was carried by a tremendous 283 to 16.

By the evening he had recovered. "Well, Henry," he said merrily to Thornton, "what shall we abolish next?"—and when someone else wanted to make a list of "those 16 miscreants," he looked up from a note he was writing on his knee and said: "Never mind the miserable 16. Think of the glorious 283!"

Actually, the struggle had only just begun. First, there would be the fight to obtain Abolition by other countries and to enforce it. Then, the battle to end slavery itself. Meanwhile, though, a tremendous victory had been won. Wilberforce, however, gave the credit elsewhere: "I cannot account for the fervour which happily now has taken the place of that fastidious well-bred lukewarmness which used to display itself on this subject, except by supposing it to be produced by the almighty power which can influence at will the judgements and affections of men."

Others recognized the human agency involved. Philosopher and public figure Sir James Mackintosh, who heard the news in Bombay, wrote, "We are apt perpetually to express our wonder that so much exertion should be necessary to suppress flagrant injustice. The more just reflection will be that a short period of the short life of one man is, when well and wisely directed, sufficient to remedy the miseries of millions for ages."

Leckey's verdict in his *History of European Morals* may still be the best: "The unweary, unostentatious and inglorious crusade of England against slavery may probably be regarded as among the three or four perfectly virtuous pages comprised in the history of nations."

In the one-and-three-quarter centuries since Abolition some have found it incredible that this great reform was initiated and carried through by men inspired by a religious motive. The most prominent is Dr. Eric Williams, later Prime Minister of Trinidad and Tobago, who in 1944 published *Capitalism and Slavery*. The gravamen of his case was that the role of the Christian abolitionists had been "seriously exaggerated by men like Sir Reginald Coupland who have sacrificed scholarship to sentimentality and placed faith before reason and evidence." In particular Dr. Williams argued that, during the Napoleonic Wars, many traditional supporters of the old system of imperial protection were deserting the West Indian interest, while there was an overproduction of British sugar in relation to available markets. The reason for Abolition was purely economic, neither the Trade nor slavery being any longer profitable.

Professor Roger Anstey has since shown in a series of books that Dr. Williams' theories are inaccurate. In fact the Trade was at its most profitable at the time of its abolition and the economic potential of the slave system was greater after Abolition than before. Nor did the over-production arguments hold water. Anstey concludes, "The Coupland school was absolutely right in stressing that behind the political activity of the religiously minded men who constituted the core of the abolitionist lobby was a theology of a profoundly dynamic kind and one which . . . had a profound significance both on the development of a theology of anti-slavery and for future social reform."

"From the assurance that their sins were forgiven through the Grace of God in the redemptive work of Christ," Dr. Anstey writes of Wilberforce and his friends, "they knew not only that they could overcome evil in their own hearts but also that they could conquer the evils in the world which they felt called to combat."

Wilberforce was well aware of the courageous work of Quakers like John Woolman and Anthony Benezet in the United States who not only worked against the Slave Trade but also against slavery itself. By the time of Woolman's death in 1772, for example, most Pennsylvanian Quakers had freed their slaves and in 1780 Pennsylvania passed an Act abolishing slavery within its boundaries.

Throughout his fight against the Trade, Wilberforce kept in close touch with developments in America. In 1804, he wrote to the future President James Monroe, who was visiting London as one of two Commissioners negotiating a commercial treaty, asking him whether he could disprove rumours that certain States in the Union had revived the Slave Trade after "prohibiting it for several years." Monroe reassured him, and the men met and became friends. Wilberforce praised the United States, saying that "without having had so much light thrown on the subject as has been cast on it here, you have seen enough to induce you to do your utmost to put a stop to this unjust trade."

During the victorious House of Lords debate in 1807 Wilberforce encouraged Grenville with the news that Congress was bringing in an Abolition Bill, which was already in Committee "without oppositon nor any anticipated." He also wrote to Monroe of his joy at "the concurrence of our two countries in carrying into execution this great work of benevolence." As it turned out, Congress passed this Bill just eight months after the British Abolition Act.

After Monroe became President ten years later, an Anglo-American Convention was signed to counter the smuggling of slaves by British slavers pretending to be American and vice versa. Both navies were authorized to free slaves they intercepted, no matter which navy rescued them or which flag the slave ship was flying.

9

State of the Nation

NOT EVEN IN THE MIDST of his titanic battle against the Slave Trade had Wilberforce forgotten the second "great object" which he believed that God had "set before" him: the reformation of the manners—or morals—of England. This was in many ways an even more formidable task than abolishing the Slave Trade and was bound to lead to equally fierce opposition, for the cultured aristocracy which governed Britain had not the faintest feeling that its manners needed reforming. They thought of their time as a very high point of civilization.

At first glance, one might be inclined to agree with them. Furneaux, for example, truly calls the late eighteenth century "a period to which we can look back with nostalgia as an age in which taste was at its highest and in which every field was dominated by a man of genius."* "The Whig aristocracy," he

*The list is indeed formidable—Pitt, Burke and Fox as statesmen, Bentham as philosopher, Gibbon as historian, Reynolds and Gainsborough as artists, Johnson as wit, Boswell as biographer, Scott as novelist, Goldsmith and Sheridan as playwrights, Garrick and Mrs. Siddons as actors, Malthus, Adam Smith and Ricardo

adds, "closely connected, supremely confident, rich in wealth and talents, are among the most attractive in our history. If we were asked in what age and class we would like to be reincarnated, we might well choose theirs. Although surrounded by every imaginable luxury and privilege, they retained an idealism, an attachment to liberty and a loathing for oppression most notably exemplified in Charles James Fox."

We have already seen how Fox fought, in and out of office, to abolish the Slave Trade and how Wilberforce, who had at first written him off as one of the most worldly of men, came to appreciate his broad humanity. Others, too, clearly measured up to Furneaux's estimate, but one doubts whether "idealism, attachment to liberty and a loathing of oppression" were really the dominant characteristics of the Whig aristocracy as a whole in the late eighteenth century. Quite apart from generally supporting the Slave Trade, most of them tolerated the increasing penury of the majority of their own countrymen with complete equanimity. Indeed, Furneaux himself points out the corruption and drunkenness endemic in even the best of them and concludes, "the rich lived in a state of selfish pagan hedonism."

The historian, John Marlowe, goes further, perhaps too far. "The venality of English political life," he writes, "was the counterpart of the coarseness and profligacy of the social life of the English governing classes. And there was a quality about it even more repellant than venality—the quality of heartlessness. There was very little to choose between the political and social morals of the English and the French aristocracy in the century before the French revolution."

What, then, was the pervading spirit of this paradoxical society in which Wilberforce found himself? It is not unsym-

---

as economists, Wesley as preacher, Wordsworth and Cowper as poets, and the Adam brothers and Nash as architects.

pathetically described by Miss Muriel Jaeger in her brilliant *Before Victoria*:

> The prevailing spirit of the English upper-class society at the time was that of a true aristocracy, "Do what you will and take the consequences" . . . There were few rules except the flexible ones of good taste. In general a man must fight a duel when challenged, and himself challenge when insulted. Everyone must meet his or her gambling debts, if no other. It was proper to be discreet in liaisons; they might be well-known to everyone in society, but they must not be flaunted . . . On the wife's side, it was incumbent on her to provide her husband with an heir of his own blood before following her own inclinations. If, as in the case of the Melbournes, the heir died and another man's son was left as legal successor, that was unfortunate, but everyone must make the best of it without fuss . . . These general rules of civilized behaviour had been imported from the salons of Paris, whence had come the pervading fashionable influence for more than a century—such a line of conduct as is set out in Lord Chesterfield's *Letters to his Son*. The famous letters, published after Chesterfield's death in 1773, received a good deal of hostile criticism. Nor was his adoption of the French custom that husband and wife should have separate establishments imitated in this country even in the highest ranks of society. However a married couple might rarely see each other in the London season and it was considered provincial, if not positively vulgar, to invite them out together . . . But if eighteenth century standards were lax, they were exacting in matters of tone and style. It was the fashion to be well-educated, to read widely, to appreciate the arts and literature, to know something of scientific developments, to have an open mind on every subject under the sun, and to discuss them all freely. Above all, it was desirable to possess that graceful insouciance which is the bloom on the cheek of a high civilization, and the heroes of society were those who best realised this ideal.

"Insouciance" was easier to achieve in high society than elsewhere and the "high civilization" looked better from above than from below; for late eighteenth-century society was built on the Slave Trade, child labour, the poverty of the masses and political corruption in high places. If society was, in Trevelyan's phrase, "one vast casino" and young men, whose fathers had acquired their fortunes through corruption, could frequently win or lose £10,000 in a night at Brooks', it was because the multitudes laboured ceaselessly without hope. In the mines, women carried coal up steep ladders in creels weighing as much as 170 pounds, taking much of the weight on a strap round their foreheads which permanently deformed them. In one typical colliery, in 1780, 173 children under seven were at work. In the mills, such children were employed thirteen, fourteen, fifteen or even sixteen hours a day. Parish overseers in London and the big towns entered into agreements to deliver them by the barge-load. "Such frightful contrasts between excess of luxury and splendour and these scenes of starvation and brutality ought not to be possible," wrote the usually cynical diarist, Charles Greville, of the Regent's England. "Before many years elapse these things will produce some great convulsion."

The theatre, although somewhat improved in performance by Garrick and others, was no longer Shakespeare's theatre of the people, but a gentleman's pastime, often valued for its side-shows. "A playhouse and the regions about it are the very hotbeds of vice," wrote Johnson's literary executor, Sir John Hawkins, in 1787. "No sooner is a playhouse open in any part of the kingdom than it at once becomes surrounded by a halo of brothels." In fact, so-called "culture" and profligacy often went hand in hand and an assumed "insouciance" too often turned into callousness towards others. The Regency bucks who spent their evenings beating up ancient night watchmen were a symptom of the times.

The poor, particularly in the cities, were often degraded and sottish. Where the statesmen "sailed on a sea of claret" (Pitt, Burke and Sheridan did not hesitate to appear drunk in the House) the poor floundered in an ocean of gin. At one point one-eighth of deaths in London were attributed to excessive drinking of spirits and women even killed their children to be able to sell their clothes for gin money. Townsfolk regularly complained of being kept awake by the screams of victims of assault and rape. The eighteenth century may have been no more vice-ridden than many others, but "no other age," writes Ian Bradley, "has ever paraded its weaknesses quite so openly or excessively."

Law and order had been a major problem throughout the century. Streets were unlit, police supervision negligible and the opportunities for crime correspondingly great. A fierce resistance to the idea of a regular police force existed, for fear that it might, as on the Continent, become a weapon of repression instead of a servant of the people; and Pitt's Metropolitan Police Bill was defeated overwhelmingly in 1785. There was little understanding in Parliament how hardly the enclosure of common land and the abolition of ancient privileges were pressing upon country folk or of how the beginning of the industrial revolution was impoverishing the workers.* The remedy to increasing crime would have been to take measures to improve the lot of the poor, and then enforce a milder penal code efficiently. The authorities, however, believed with Malthus that natural economic forces should not be interfered with and with Locke that the preservation of private property was the Government's prime purpose and the foundation of the individual's freedom in the face of the executive. They concluded that, if crime increased, the law must be insufficiently deterrent. More and more laws were

---

*One evening in 1795, after discoursing to a friend in Essex of the good fortune which an industrious and virtuous labourer could enjoy in Britain, William Pitt was taken by his host to see the houses of the poor in the town of Halstead. "The Minister," relates his biographer, Lord Rosebery, "surveyed it in silent wonder, and declared he had no conception that any part of England could present a spectacle of such misery."

passed imposing the death penalty for ever more minor offences.

In 1688 there were only some thirty capital offences. In 1765 Blackstone put the number at 160 and by 1800 this had increased again to over 200. Thus one Act imposed the death penalty for the theft of hares, rabbits, fish, for cutting down trees, wounding cattle, or setting fire to any house, barn, haystack or wood. The penalty could be applied equally to men, women and children over fourteen—and in some cases to children over seven. "There is probably no country in the world in which so many and so great a variety of human actions are punishable with loss of life as in England," wrote Romilly in the year of Wilberforce's conversion.

Established religion was little or no help in the situation. The Church of England was primarily a department of state responsible for ecclesiastical affairs—and the maintenance of the status quo. At a time when Government majorities in the House of Lords were ensured by an adroit use of patronage, bishops were chosen for political, not spiritual, reasons. Their twenty-six votes in an average attendance of one hundred and twenty were an important factor; and they were expected to vote with the Government of the day and to stay in London eight months in the year to do so. In their dioceses, they were expected to be a centre of loyalty and propaganda, but their effect was limited because the Church had lost touch with the industrial masses.

Dr. Johnson stated roundly on Good Friday, 1775, that "no man can now be made a bishop for his learning or piety; his only chance of promotion is his being connected with someone with a parliamentary interest." Thus Pitt appointed his old Cambridge tutor, George Pretyman, Bishop first of Lincoln and later of London, while Dr. Richard Watson was elevated to the See of Llandaff because he had written a pamphlet about America which happened to support Lord Shelburne's policy. Bishop Watson preferred, however, to live beside Lake Windermere, 300 miles away from his diocese. The Bishops in their turn filled their dioceses with their family and friends. When Bishop Sparke reigned at Ely, it was said that you could find your way across the fens at night by the light of all the little Sparkes shining in their parsonages. At the time when Wilberforce was considering how to reform the manners of England, it was calculated that 7,000 out of the 11,000 clergy did not live in their parishes. Others were what he called "buck parsons," spending their time in hunting and high living rather than the care of their flocks.

There were of course saintly men here and there as well as good shepherds and great scholars, and at least the clergy did not seem, by and large, to have adopted the sexual mores of the aristocracy. In other matters, however, many conformed to the customs of the times. Nepotism was rife and the most nepotic of all the century's Archbishops of Canterbury was John Moore (1783-1805), the one with whom Wilberforce had to deal. Archbishop Moore secured well-feathered nests for five sons, three as Joint-Registrars of the Prerogative Court of Canterbury and the other two as Joint-Registrars of the Vicar-General's Office. One received not less than £12,000 a year for fifty years, at a time when missionaries to the Indians in North America were paid between £10 and £30 a year and over 4,000 English clergy between £50 and £150.

"It is extremely difficult," writes Overton, the distinguished historian of the eighteenth-century Church, "for any man to rise above the spirit of his age. He who can do so is a spiritual hero . . . It surely does not follow that because a man cannot be a hero he must therefore be a bad man." This apologia may be true enough, but it is hardly surprising that followers of Christ who failed to rise above their age as conspicuously as most of its prelates should feel it hard to understand men like John Wesley. Hardly any episcopal "charge" between 1740 and 1780 failed to condemn him.

Nevertheless the awakening so improbably initiated by the quiet Oxford don, together with his brother Charles and George Whitefield, swept through the lower—and increasingly the middle—classes. In the fifty years preceding Wilberforce's conversion, John Wesley alone had travelled 225,000 miles up and down the kingdom, mostly on horseback, and preached more than 50,000 sermons in halls, at fairs, in military camps, on any open space where he could gain a hearing. The 700 full-time lay preachers working with him in the 1780s (almost all "unlearned men" in the eyes of the bishops) were scarcely less active. For them "no weather was too inclement, no road too boggy, no ford too swollen, no community too degraded, no privation too severe." One travelled not less than 100,000 miles on one horse. Another, his horse worn out, walked 1,200 miles in one winter. All were persecuted as were the Wesleys themselves: some being killed by mobs, others carried off by press gangs, many having their houses burnt over them, while the clergy and local big-wigs often egged on the attackers. But tens of thousands of lives had been changed by a faith which, in Overton's words, "made selfish men self-denying, the discontented happy, the worldling spiritually minded, the drunkard sober, the sexual chaste, the liar truthful, the thief honest, the proud humble, the godless godly, the thriftless thrifty."

As the century proceeded, the awakening worked its way upward in society and George Whitefield in particular interested some and converted a few among the aristocracy. He was powerfully aided by his patroness, Selina, Countess of Huntingdon. His and the Countess's converts in high society were, however, generally regarded as cranks.

Such was the situation with which Wilberforce was faced as he set out to "reform the manners of England." It was a formidable task for a man of twenty-seven, even though he was the Prime Minister's best friend, the Member for Yorkshire and one of the ablest speakers in the House of Commons. How was he to go about it?

Facing facts, he had to admit that neither penal reform, nor a Christian revival among the rich looked immediately in prospect. A more practical aim in 1786 seemed to be to try to restore the respect for the law in all classes and to find a way of making goodness, instead of evil, fashionable among the ruling classes. The ultimate answer was the kind of change of heart which had come to him and Eliot and others. But for the moment something wider than personal conversion was needed.

"The barbarous custom of hanging," he wrote to Wyvill," has been tried for too long, and with the success that might have been expected. The most effectual way to prevent the greater crimes is by punishing the smaller, and by endeavouring to repress the general spirit of licentiousness, which is the parent of every kind of vice." He admitted that "regulating the outward conduct did not change the hearts of men," but at least the obtrusiveness of temptation could be removed and this would help.

To Dudley Ryder he added: "Don't imagine that I am about to run amuck and tilt at all I meet. You know that on many grounds I am a sworn enemy to the Clubs, but I don't think of opening my trenches to them and commencing open war on such potent adversaries. But then I honestly confess to you that I am restrained only by the conviction that by such desperate measures I should injure rather than serve the Cause I have in view, and whenever prudential motives do not repress my "noble rage" I would willingly hunt down vice whether in St. James or St. Giles's."

Wilberforce knew that by attempting to change the manners of England, he would encounter ridicule and suspicion. He hoped nevertheless that, by promoting a greater respect for the law, he would cheat the gallows of many poor wretches and make Parliament more ready for penal reform. He hoped too that many of the ruling classes, even if they would not immediately change their whole lives as Eliot or Thornton had done, would be shamed into better conduct. Others, he hoped, might no longer feel the need to pretend that they were worse than they really were, for he believed that hypocrisy could run in more directions than one.

"When a profession of Religion opens the road to respect and power," he added in his letter to Dudley Ryder, "there is always a great deal of religious hypocrisy; we have now an hypocrisy of an opposite sort, and I believe many affect to be worse than in principle they really are, out of deference to the licentious moral [sic] of the fashionable world."

10

The Reformation of Manners

IT WAS A HIERARCHICAL AGE. For all the ordinary gentleman's sturdy independence—the farmer who ordered George III, a popular monarch, off his land was a national hero—society was set in a known and respected pyramid. Wilberforce knew that he would get nowhere in his campaign to "reform the manners" of the country unless he procured powerful sponsorship. So his first step was to induce George III to reissue the "Proclamation for the Encouragement of Piety and Virtue and for the Preventing of Vice, Profaneness and Immorality," which he, like every British king of the century, had issued on his accession in 1760.

Such Proclamations were usually formal statements, which were promptly ignored. But Wilberforce had discovered that the one issued by William and Mary had had a real effect, because it was followed up by the formation of local Societies for the Reformation of Manners. These Societies helped the magistrates in detecting crime but also in setting an example. The House of Commons appointed a committee for this latter purpose. Under the Hanoverians, however, in Pollock's words, "the libertines regained the initiative."

After consulting Bishop Porteous, Wilberforce put his idea to Pitt who gave his "entire approbation" to Archbishop Moore and to the Queen. Moore apparently talked to the King and the Proclamation was reissued on June 1st, 1787. Few realized, at first, that the young Member for Yorkshire had had anything to do with it, for he disguised matters with an "amiable confusion."

The Proclamation followed the traditional form as drafted in 1692 and as reissued by George III on his accession, except for a long Preamble, referring to the King's concern at "the rapid progress of impiety and licentiousness, and that deluge of profaneness, immorality and every kind of vice which to the scandal of our holy religion, and to the evil example of our loving subjects, have broken upon this nation: We, therefore . . . have thought fit, by the advice of our Privy Council, to issue this our Royal Proclamation, and do hereby declare our Royal purpose and resolution to discountenance and punish all manner of vice, profaneness and immorality, in all persons of whatever degree or quality, within this Realm, and particularly in such as are employed near our Royal Person. . . ." The eight paragraphs which followed were the traditional ones. If applied literally, they would transform the England—and not least the High Society—of 1787 or any other age.

The first prescribed that all people of honour or authority should set a good example themselves and help reform "persons of dissolute and debauched lives." The King's subjects were forbidden to play cards or dice on the Lord's Day and should attend divine worship. Judges, sheriffs and justices were to be "very vigilant and strict in the discovery and eventual prosecution of all persons who should be guilty of excessive drinking, blasphemy, profane swearing and cursing, lewdness, or other immoral and dissolute practices" and must suppress disorderly houses and "all loose and licentious prints, books and publications dispersing poison in the minds of the young and unwary and to punish the publishers and vendors thereof. . . ."

The Secretary of State at the Home Department was instructed to send six copies of the Proclamation to the High Sheriff of every county, with the King's command that it be carried into effect.

Wilberforce was now ready to initiate the second part of his plan: the setting up of a Proclamation Society in the hope that, as in the days of William and Mary, the Proclamation might become a force rather than a farce. In those days the Crown seldom prosecuted. That was left to the victim of a crime or to a private person—a most important fact in understanding Wilberforce's actions. He puzzled how to deal with legal offences which were not directed against the person or property, but against the common good; offences widely practised but universally agreed in that age to be the seedbed of more serious crime. A Society governed by responsible people, would, he considered, be most likely to avoid malicious prosecutions and less liable to encounter charges of slander than if such matters were left to any busybody. Also it had the side effect of challenging those who took up such responsibilities to match their conduct to their words.

On June 7th, therefore, Wilberforce called on the Duke of Montagu, the Master of the Horse, and asked him "to be president of a society for carrying into execution the proclamation of last Sunday's *Gazette*." On June 13th, he explained the plan further to Montagu's brother, Lord Ailesbury, who recorded, "He proposes certain rules which arise out of the proclamation and a committee of five persons, one of which was Sir Charles Middleton. . . ." In fact, no gathering of this small committee took place until November—for Wilberforce was against any dramatic announcements—and on that occasion it consisted, besides Middleton and himself, of Edward Eliot and the bishops of Lincoln (Pitt's former tutor, Pretyman), Salisbury (Barrington) and London (Porteous, who had just been translated from Chester). Only six dukes, eleven lesser peers, nineteen archbishops and bishops and a dozen commoners were invited to the first meeting of the full Society, and Wilberforce told one of them, "Nothing is to be announced to the world of society, only that the gentlemen mentioned have felt the necessity of attending to His Majesty's call and have agreed to assist in carrying the Proclamation into effect." The reforming movement was not specifically religious, and Wilberforce did not try only to enlist the religious or even the moderately moral. Some of the grandees he approached and whose support he gained were in fact notoriously dissolute. But the guts of the movement, the engine within the car, to use a modern metaphor, were men and women of religion, people like Edward Eliot, Middleton and Hannah More, and a little later the Henry Thorntons and the John Venns, and others who had gathered round him.

Right through the summer of 1787, Wilberforce was active telling people about his plan. He early obtained Bishop Pretyman's support in spite of the Bishop's dislike of the kind of religion which Wilberforce represented, and the Duke of Manchester, a man of not quite spotless reputation, expressed himself as particularly keen that young and humane men like Wilberforce should strive to reduce the horrifying number of hangings by a rise of moral standards and working towards a revision of the penal code. When the House rose, Wilberforce hurtled up and down the dusty roads of England, calling on the great men of the provinces. He even tried to enlist his old adversary, Lord Fitzwilliam, who laughed in his face, allowing that there was much debauchery and very little religion, but that this was inevitable in a rich nation. "The only way to reform morals is to ruin purses," Lord Fitzwilliam said, adding that he feared that such a Society would lead to another round of Gordon Riots. Another nobleman simply led Wilberforce to a painting of the Crucifixion to show him the common fate of young reformers. Horace Walpole* blandly remarked that the

---

*Son of Prime Minister Sir Robert Walpole, author and wit.

Proclamation was "no more minded in Town than St. Swithin's Day."

Indeed London society was not transformed overnight, nor had Wilberforce expected it to be. He had however called the Establishment's bluff by involving them in a bid to reshape the nation's (and their own) conduct in line with the often-stated but seldom practised principles of the age.

The time must have been riper for change than Horace Walpole imagined, for magistrates in many parts of the country responded to the Proclamation eagerly. Perhaps it was the seriousness of the crime rate which enlisted people; and the underlying strength of the thousands whose lives and conduct had been changed through Wesley's awakening and its many offshoots played a large part. There were meetings everywhere to consider how the Proclamation could be carried into effect, and parish officers, constables and churchwardens were specially briefed on the long-existing but unenforced law. Licences which had been granted year after year for adequate consideration to disorderly houses were suddenly refused, and public houses, which had been allowed to stay open all night, were closed at nine or ten and completely on Sundays. A new kind of magistrate began to appear, and the corrupt "trading magistrates," portrayed in the novels of Smollett and Fielding, increasingly disappeared. After 1802, when the Society for the Suppression of Vice took the place of the Proclamation Society, the clean-up became even fiercer. Within a year of its foundation 678 offenders were brought before the courts.

Not everyone welcomed its activities. As informers were inevitably encouraged—though Wilberforce himself always opposed their payment and strove against convictions by deceit—there was sometimes good reason for criticism. Prosecutions of the few, if often brutal, pleasures of the poor (bull-baiting and cockfighting, for example), while the rich did as they pleased, naturally caused anger. The editor and cleric Sydney Smith, in a brilliant indictment, renamed the 1802 Society "the Society for the Suppression of Vice among those with less than five hundred pounds a year."

Wilberforce and his friends had foreseen this danger and were campaigning against it. "If the Rich and the Great will not, from a liberal spirit of doing right or from a Christian spirit of fearing God, abstain from offences for which the poor are to suffer fines and imprisonment, effectual good can not be done," wrote Hannah More. And indeed the first two broadsides from her "methodical battery on vice and error," like Wilberforce's own *Practical View* and Gisborne's *An Enquiry into the Duties of Men in the Upper and Middle Classes of Society*, were directly aimed at the rich and powerful, not the poor. Her two first books were entitled *Thoughts on the Manners of the Great* and *An Estimate of the Religion of the Fashionable World* and were runaway bestsellers. "To expect to reform the poor while the opulent are corrupt," she wrote, "is to throw odours on the stream, while the springs are poisoned." "By far the greatest part of the Evangelicals' effort to extend their own concept of proper behaviour to others was directed at the middle and upper classes," writes Bradley.

Amazingly, the appeal was heeded. As early as 1798 the Annual Register noted that the approaches to churches had begun to be filled with carriages, while Wilberforce's systematic assault on the Church itself began to bear fruit. In 1813 he wrote that "the race of buck parsons is almost extinct," and by the late 1820s Gladstone estimated that an eighth of the Anglican clergy were of Wilberforce's persuasion. In 1824 a visitor to Lord Derby's home reported that "many hours were spent in Lady Derby's sitting room in scriptural investigation," and in 1840 John Stuart Mill reported that "the daily actions of every peer and peeress" were more and more affected. "They feel every day a stronger necessity of showing an immaculate front to the world," Mill wrote. By the middle of the century the Lord Lieutenant of Staffordshire reported that, whereas when he came of age only two landed gentlemen in the county held family prayers, there were now only two who did not. It has been reckoned that by then scarcely a hundred upperclass families remained anywhere in which at least one member had not undergone "the great change."

High society was also infiltrated from another angle. More and more servants and governesses took a new spirit to the younger generation. Thus the future Lord Shaftesbury, entirely neglected by his choleric father and fashion-loving mother, was set on his life's path by their Methodist housekeeper, his beloved Maria. Similarly, Selina Trimmer, the daughter of one of Wilberforce's Clapham friends, became governess to the Duchess of Devonshire's household, a typical aristocratic establishment of the period, set at the very pinnacle of society. The heart of this home was a *ménage à trois*, consisting of the Duke, the Duchess and Lady Elizabeth Foster. Others present included the three children of the Duke and Duchess, two children of the Duke and Lady Elizabeth, and two older legitimate sons of Lady Elizabeth and Caroline Ponsonby, the Duchess's niece. "The emotional disorder of life beneath the drawing-room chandeliers—the Duchess and her friend usually involved in, and in fact constantly wretched from, either debts or complicated love affairs—was reflected in the disorder in the nursery floor above, where daily existence was a mixture of luxury and scrimmage," comments a modern writer.

Such was Selina Trimmer's unlikely flock, round the fringes of which, as the girls grew up, hovered the Lamb boys, composing mocking couplets about the guarding dragon. Many and varied were the adventures of governess and children—the disastrous marriage of William Lamb* and Caroline Ponsonby being the worst tragedy amongst them. In sum, however, it can be said that most of the children, made wretched by the insecurities of their "enlightened" home, turned more and more to Selina and determined that their own children should live in different conditions.

The same happened with other families. Indeed the younger generation grasped the new ideas with such speed and enthusiasm that as early as 1810 Wilberforce was warning

*Later Lord Melbourne, Queen Victoria's first Prime Minister.

young people in the *Christian Observer* not to antagonize parents through zeal not sufficiently tempered by prudence and charity. The Princess Victoria was one of the young people indirectly affected, for the Duke of Kent chose an Evangelical clergyman as her tutor. By the time she came to the throne there were many young ladies of good family practising these new ideas, and the tutor's daughter, Mary Davys, found on arrival at Court that several of the Queen's ladies were meeting for prayer each morning before breakfast in Lady Barham's rooms. One such young lady even caught and reformed the notorious Earl of Waterford, the leader of rowdies who in the first years of the reign terrorized the approaches to London as "springheeled Jack," and who thereafter, until his death in the hunting field fifteen years later, found himself reading a chapter of the Bible each day to his Louisa. Another, Annabella Milbanke, who, although she did not love him, accepted Lord Byron's proposal of marriage in 1812 and remained with him for a year in the hope of converting him, was less successful.

Meanwhile active measures were being taken to reach the lower classes. Here the principal medium was the cheap tract or broadsheet. The tactic originated with Hannah More who in consultation with Wilberforce began in 1793 to publish *Village Politics* by Will Chip—Will Chip being a character of her own invention whose homely philosophy caught the fancy of the poorer classes and sold prodigiously at a negligible price. Distribution was skilfully organized by Henry Thornton, and in the first year of the Cheap Repository Tracts, as they were called, two million books were sold. Pedlars took them to the furthest corners of Britain and they became "the principal part of many an English Cottager's library." Thornton here shrewdly killed two birds with one stone. For, by paying them more, he took over the distribution network provided by the hawkers of obscene ballads. Other Evangelical writers followed Hannah More's example, among them Legh Richmond, after his conversion through reading Wilberforce's *Practical View*. It was his most popular work, *The Dairyman's*

Daughter, which Princess Victoria was reading to her mother when a tourist came upon them in a churchyard in the Isle of Wight in 1833. By its fiftieth anniversary, the Religious Tract Society claimed to have circulated over 500 million copies of 5,000 different titles, and to be sending out some 20 million copies a year. Not many were great literature, but they had an enormous influence.

Much of this was in the future, but already in Wilberforce's lifetime a fresh breeze was blowing away a deal of dirt and heartlessness from countless corners of national life. The initiatives which he and his friends set in motion—the Evangelical movement was unique in being led by laymen—naturally took time to work through the national life, but few would deny that he had, in fact, set on foot the "reformation of the manners" of which he had dreamed. Professor Henry Perkins, in his *Origins of Modern English Society* (1969), states that "between 1780 and 1850 the English ceased to be one of the most aggressive, brutal, rowdy, outspoken, riotous, cruel and bloodthirsty nations in the world, and became one of the most inhibited, polite, orderly, tender-minded, prudish and hypocritical." David Newsome rated evangelicalism as "perhaps the most formative power behind the eminence of eminent Victorians" and Eric Stokes described it simply as "the rock upon which the character of the Nineteenth Century Englishman was founded."

11

Serenity under Fire

LIKE ALL REFORMERS WHO challenge the existing order of things, Wilberforce came in for attack and abuse. Then, as now, character assassination was a ready weapon for the unscrupulous. While he was still a bachelor, it was widely whispered that Wilberforce was a wife-beater—and that his wife was a Black. Others declared that he was a republican and a revolutionary. "All abolitionists are Jacobins," said Lord Abingdon at the height of the French wars, and it was this smear which finally turned George III against Abolition. In the first days of the crusade the King, who was a fundamentally kindly man, whispered, "How do your black clients, Mr. Wilberforce?" but in 1792, and again in 1795, he cut Wilberforce at the Levee. "I always told Mr. Pitt they were hypocrites and not to be trusted," he told his Home Secretary, Lord Portland, in that year.

The King's sons were united with him in this as in little else. The Prince of Wales pronounced Wilberforce "Republican at heart," while the Duke of Clarence asserted in the House of Lords that "the promoters of the Abolition were either frauds or hypocrites, and in one of those classes he ranked Mr. Wilberforce." The Duke drew his views from his observations while with the Navy in Jamaica where, on his own admission, he had lived "a terrible debauched life." Boswell, who had been one of the earliest to recognize Wilberforce's abilities, now wrote:

Go, W-, with narrow skull,
Go home and preach away at Hull.
No longer to the senate cackle
In strains that suit the tabernacle,
I hate your little wittling sneer,
Your pert and self-sufficient leer,
Mischief to trade sits on your lips,
Insects will gnaw the noblest ships.
Go, W-, begone, for shame,
Thou dwarf with big resounding name.

Had Boswell just mounted the fashionable anti-Abolition bandwagon? Or was it Wilberforce's stand for Christian morality which disturbed the famous philanderer? Wilberforce had had a "serious talk" with him in 1792 and perhaps he saw himself in the "sober sensualist" of Wilberforce's *Practical View*. For many "the reformation of manners" struck nearer home than the abolition of any trade.

Every revolt or possible revolt in the West Indies was laid at Wilberforce's door. "If anything (i.e. rioting) happens to our island, I should certainly, if I was a planter, insist on Mr. Wilberforce being punished capitally," declared Lady Malmesbury in 1791, and as late as 1816, when there was a quickly suppressed slave revolt in Barbados, Langford Lovel Hodge, the Codrington agent in the island, wrote, "Mr. Wilberforce and his adherents . . . have created a volcano. Indeed I believe these calamities will be to them sources of real pleasure." This rising was followed by several violent attacks on Wilberforce, including two scurrilous pamphlets by Joseph Marryat, the MP for Sandwich and London agent for the island of Granada. The charge of inciting insurrection particularly grieved Wilberforce, for he had, in this case, been deliberately refraining from public agitation on behalf of the slaves' miseries. As was his custom, however, he made no reply.

Sometimes the attacks were more jocular. Thus, in the Commons in 1793, Lord Carhampton suggested that Wilberforce was a little addled through concentration on one subject for so long. "He therefore advised him to brush up his person a little, send for a hair-dresser, put a few curls on those straight locks, go to the play—first to Covent Garden, then to Drury Lane—and in time he should be glad to have the pleasure of seeing him with a female friend under his arm strolling at night round Covent Garden." According to several MPs present, Wilberforce took this patiently and turned the laugh "with a degree of wit, gaiety and good humour which delighted the whole House."

Almost the only recorded occasion on which Wilberforce allowed himself a resort to the devastating repartee so famous in his first years in Parliament was in 1817. In one of the Habeas Corpus debates, the radical Member, Sir Francis Burdett, referred with weighty sarcasm to his astonishment "at the concurrence in this measure of an honourable *and religious* gentleman who lays claim to a superior piety . . .", a phrase which he used again and again, tauntingly, in gross defiance of parliamentary rules. Wilberforce had not intended to speak, but rose and remarked that the Member for Westminster was "greatly mistaken if he thought that the sarcasm he used did not injure himself rather than others."

Then he proceeded to pour out what Brougham* (who supported Burdett on the measure, but not his manner) described as "a strain of sarcasm which none who heard it can ever forget":

How can the honourable member talk thus of those religious principles on which the welfare of the community depends? I would fain believe that he desires as sincerely as I do myself

---

*MP for Knaresborough, later Lord Chancellor.

to perpetuate to his country the blessings she enjoys. But if I could be base enough to seek the destruction of those institutions which we both profess to revere, I would tell him what instrument I would choose. I would take a man of great wealth, of patrician family, of personal popularity, aye and of respectable talents, and I am satisfied that such a one, while he scattered abroad the firebrands of sedition under pretence that he went all lengths for the people, would in reality be the best agent in the malevolent purpose of destroying their liberties and happiness.

Burdett sat on a bench above and behind Wilberforce, and Members opposite could see him, his back stiff with anger, above Wilberforce's tiny figure. But when Wilberforce turned and spoke direct to Burdett, Acland thought it "like a giant dangling a dwarf." "It is the most striking thing I almost ever heard," Romilly commented when a member remarked to him that Wilberforce had excelled even Pitt, the acknowledged master of sarcasm. "But," added Romilly, "I look upon it as a more singular proof of Wilberforce's virtue than of his genius, for who but he ever possessed such a formidable weapon, and never used it!"

Thomas Buxton, Wilberforce's chosen successor for the Emancipation fight, spoke of this restraint: "Often during a debate he would whisper to me hints and witticisms which would have filled the House with merriment and overwhelmed the opponent. But when he rose to speak, though he went close to the very thoughts he had poured into my ear, he restrained himself from uttering them, nor would he ever give vent to any allusion which might give another pain."

Wilberforce consistently maintained that restraint. After a particularly scurrilous attack in the *Courier* he commented, "I am rather animated than discouraged by it." "Remember," he said to Macaulay* on another occasion, "that they will by-and-

---

*Zachary Macaulay, see Chapter 12.

by appear only like the barking of cottage curs on our passing through a village, when on our progress in the journey of life." He much preferred curses to sycophancy. "I had rather he had spat in my face," he said of one flatterer. Disappointment did sometimes assail him when, year after year, the cause he was campaigning for was worsted in the House of Commons, yet he never lost hope. What was it that enabled him to retain his serenity?

In the first place he was armoured against calumny by the totality of his first decision. When his brother Charles was fussing about an assault on his reputation, John Wesley remarked, "Brother, when I devoted to God my ease, my time, my life, did I except my reputation?" In the same way Wilberforce, by visiting the "Methodist" John Newton after his week-long struggle in November 1785, had finally given God his reputation. He had once and for all decided to identify himself with the keenest, and so most spoken against, spiritual force of his times. That commitment largely freed him from the fear of men's opinions.

It was a commitment sustained by the discipline of Wilberforce's life. Through all the years, but particularly in the early ones, his journal chronicles daily struggles. He kept a sharp watch on himself. In 1788 he made a daily chart showing exactly how his time had been spent: how much with God (half an hour to one and a half hours daily, much more on Sundays), how much on work, what in bed, what "squandered." He sought to discipline tongue, tastes and thoughts equally. "He was not labouring to reduce intemperate habits within the limits of that self-indulgent propriety which contents the generality of men," comment his sons. "It was his object to gain such control over his lower nature, that it should never impede his usefulness in social intercourse, or clog the freedom of his communings with God."

He knew the value of the first hours of the day: "In the calmness of the morning before the mind is heated and weary by the turmoil of the day, you have a season of unusual importance for communing with God and with yourself." In the day-to-day battle it was, more and more, these early morning hours (kept up in spite of late nights and chronic ill-health) and his quiet Sundays which gave him strength and perspective on himself and the world.

In 1801, for example, when a "Peace Government" under Addington was installed, many felt that Wilberforce would be included. He was, he admitted, "for a little intoxicated and had risings of ambition." Sunday brought the cure. "Blessed be to God for the day of rest and religious occupation wherein earthly things assume their true size. Ambition is stunted . . ." runs the journal. He was not included, nor could have been with his inconvenient convictions. To understand his victory over himself one needs to remember, with Trevelyan, that Wilberforce "could probably have been Pitt's successor as Prime Minister if he had preferred party to mankind."

He recommended such times of reflection to many. To an over-busy man of affairs, he said, "I have always found that I have the most time for business, and it is best done, when I have most properly observed my private devotions"—a remark which reminds one of St. Francis de Sales' advice on a similar occasion that "half an hour's daily listening to God is essential, except when you are very busy. Then a full hour is needed." "Poor fellow," was Wilberforce's frequent worry about Pitt, "he never schools his mind by a cessation from political ruminations, the most blinding, hardening and souring of all others." To this same lack he attributed the suicides of Romilly and Castlereagh. With peaceful Sundays, "the strings would never have snapped as they did from overtension."

Anyone who is familiar with the pressures under which politicians work today, whether in Washington, London or elsewhere, and has heard Cabinet Ministers say that they have had no time to think since they assumed office, must feel that Wilberforce had discovered an important secret. The pressures in a modern capital may be greater, but he himself survived fifty years of exceptionally busy public life, in spite of his "calico guts," his impaired eyesight and the steel brace which he secretly wore to support his tiny frame. There were no typewriters in those days, and he had to write most of his myriad letters by hand. Indeed, it was considered insulting to address an equal—and he was a mere commoner—on all but the most formal matters except in one's own hand. Moreover, in his "Noah's Ark" he was more vulnerable to every contact than is the modern Congressman or Member of Parliament, let alone a Minister with his vigilant staff.

Wilberforce believed that God could give a man detailed guidance, that He could put a thought into a man's mind, in exactly the same way as He did to the prophets in the Old Testament or to Paul, Ananias, and a score of others in the Acts of the Apostles. He once asked a visiting clergyman if he believed in "particular providence."

"Yes, on Great Occasions," his visitor replied.

"As unphilosophical as unscriptural," commented Wilberforce. "Must not the smallest links be as necessary for maintaining the continuity as the greatest? Great and little belong to our littleness, but there is no great or little to God."

He also believed in a Providence which intervened in both personal and national affairs. Furneaux finds it hard to explain how practical men like Wilberforce and Thornton could hold such a belief and remarks that the workings of Providence were puzzling. "Wilberforce claimed that the successful vote in the Commons on the Indian Missions in 1793 was the clearest example of intervention he had ever seen," he writes. "The Court of Directors at once rallied their forces and threw out the motion. Wilberforce did not speculate as to whether Providence might have changed its mind. Again, when Henry Thornton was dying, Wilberforce wrote, 'The sudden removal of such a man would be a most mysterious providence.' He allowed Providence to have the best of both worlds."*

*Such arguments remind one a little of the querulous letters to *The Times* when, in 1978, the Cardinals elected John Paul I only for him to die seventeen days later. "How could the Holy Spirit be supposed to have inspired that election?" the

True enough, but one fancies that Wilberforce would again answer, "As unphilosophical as unscriptural." Certainly the Bible is full of people who shared Wilberforce's approach, people who were not so much trying to construct a watertight theology as to learn to live more trustfully with a God who was wiser than they. Certainly, too, that reliance, through good and ill, on a wise God lay at the root of Wilberforce's serenity. He did all that he could and then left the result in God's hands. Otherwise, he could not have survived so many disappointments. His faith was resilient because it was not in himself but, as he said after one of his defeats, in God "who has given the very small increase there has been so far and must give all if there be more."

correspondents asked. Would anyone doubt today that Pope John Paul I's short papacy was blessed or that a Polish Pope could have been elected without it?

12

The Clapham Community

THERE WAS ANOTHER REASON for Wilberforce's astonishing persistence and steadiness in his campaigns; he never worked alone. He was sustained, from the earliest days after taking them on, by a varied and growing group of friends who gathered round him. Those who worked with him in Parliament, like Eliot and Henry Thornton, became known, at first derisively but with mounting, if secret, admiration as "The Saints."

It began as an entirely informal body of friends drawn together by shared views and a common aim. Then in 1792, when the battles against the Trade and for the reformation of manners were well under way, the arrangement took on a somewhat more definite shape. In that year Henry Thornton suggested to Wilberforce that the two of them set up a "chummery" in Clapham, in and around Battersea Rise, the sturdy Queen Anne house on the West side of the Common which he had bought after his father's death. Clapham, then a village and only four miles south of Westminster, was convenient enough, and thus was formed the basis of the community which, quite incorrectly and only after their deaths, became known as the Clapham sect.*

Like most of Thornton's schemes, it was a carefully premeditated affair. He felt that living together in such a community would much facilitate "The Saints"'twin aims of a deeper personal commitment and a more concerted influence on affairs. "On the whole," he wrote to Charles Grant in 1793, "I am in hopes that some good may come out of our Clapham system. Mr. Wilberforce is a candle that should not be hid under a bushel. The influence of his conversation is great and striking . . . I am not surprised to find how much religion everybody seems to have when they get into our house."

Battersea Rise proved to be an ideal centre for such a community of friends, some of whom lived there, while others came to stay for short or long periods. Thornton added several wings to the house, until it eventually had 34 bedrooms, as well as a magnificent oval library designed by Pitt, which was, until Thornton's death in 1815, the "cabinet room" and general centre of the community. In the extensive gardens he also built two smaller houses, Broomfield Lodge, which was rented by Edward Eliot and after his death by Wilberforce, and Glenelg which was bought by Charles Grant. Grant was an entrepreneur who had returned from India in 1790 and had since become both Member of Parliament for Invernessshire and a Director of the East India Company. Eliot and he were established in their new houses by 1794, and the lawns, shaded by elms, firs and tulip trees, stretched continuously between the three houses without hedge or hindrance.

By that time a strong nucleus had already gathered in Clapham, since a number of other friends had already made their homes there. Henry's two elder brothers, both Members of Parliament, lived on in the nearby family estate; Evangeli-

---

*The name "Clapham Sect" was not used till twelve years after Wilberforce's death and thirty years after Clapham had ceased to be the centre of "The Saints'" activities. It was doubly misleading as they were never anything like a sect and their fellowship was always nationwide—and, indeed, stretched far beyond Britain.

cals, but a little aloof from the active core. Granville Sharp, twenty years their elder and the man who forced Chief Justice Mansfield to free the slaves within Britain, and William Smith, the Unitarian and Radical MP, already lived in the village. And as the years went by others joined them. James Stephen, Master-in-Chancery and MP for Tralee and East Grinstead successively, had a house across the Green. Zachary Macaulay, who had been a slave-overseer and estate manager before his conversion,* settled in the High Street with his wife Selina Miles when he returned from being Governor of Sierra Leone. Charles Grant's intimate friend, John Shore, now Lord Teignmouth, joined them when he retired from being Governor-General of India in 1802.

There was also a stream of visitors, who included Wilberforce's old St. John's friends, Babington and Gisborne, Hannah More, poet, pamphleteer and playwright; Charles Simeon of Cambridge, whose sway in the Church became, according to Lord Macaulay, "greater than any primate's," and Dean Milner.

Meanwhile, the Thorntons, in whose gift was the living of Clapham, had acquired John Venn, the son of one of the pioneers of evangelicalism and himself a great preacher and wise counsellor, as their parson.

Such was the nucleus which gathered round Wilberforce and sustained him in his struggles as he did in theirs. They were "a group whose brains could not be denied, even by those who sneered at their religion," and they possessed between them an astonishing range of capacities: encyclopaedic knowledge ("Look it up in Macaulay" was a common cry), a capacity for research, sparkling wit and literary style, business sagacity, intimate knowledge of India and the West Indies,

---

*Returning to England, sickened by slavery but unregenerate enough to fleece several skilled gamblers at cards on the ship, he found his sister married to Babington, which led to his conversion. He was an invaluable recruit. "Denied," according to his great nephew, Sir G. O. Trevelyan, "of any sense of the ridiculous," he was an amazingly swift and thorough worker, getting to the heart of a document faster than any of his friends.

legal ability, oratory and parliamentary skill. "No Prime Minister," comments one historian, "had such a cabinet as Wilberforce could summon to his assistance."

The Clapham men and their families lived together as a true community. They strolled into each others' homes uninvited and seem always to have been welcome. Even on what Lady Knutsford said "may ironically be called their holidays," they frequented the same watering places, or turned up at each others' country houses. In fact they lived, worked and planned together in a kind of permanent committee. Sometimes it was just useful chat, as when Thornton noted in his spasmodic diary: "Talked with Wilber a few hours on politics gaining much information from him . . . Hurried off to dine with Wilber and Dr. Milner—talked two to three hours." Sometimes they met for those friendly times of self-criticism which Wilberforce, Babington and Thornton valued so highly. Often they gathered in "Cabinet Councils" in Thornton's library over the public cause or personal needs of the moment, for private as well as public plans were common property between them. They aimed to make every decision on a basis of what, as far as they could see, God desired for the whole fellowship and for the country; they believed this perspective was not best found alone. So, "Decided with Grant and Thornton" or "Cabinet Council with Stephen, Thornton and Macaulay" became the frequent entries in Wilberforce's diaries. When is it right to go into Yorkshire? Should I move from Clapham to Kensington Gore? Do I give up the county seat? In these and many other decisions he naturally consulted his friends and they him.

They were, then, bound together by a common commitment and way of life. They did not all agree on all points of theology—far from it. As Hannah More wrote of Thornton: "It is not for doctrine I esteem him but for living, while in the luxury of the world, in that heroic self-denial and communion with God which makes him the most impressive example I ever saw." The fact was that each had, in his own way, been through an experience of rebirth similar to that which had transformed Wilberforce. We have seen how Henry Thornton was rescued from cynicism and how Eliot, the "Sir Bull" of Goosetrees, had become a different man. James Stephen, the lawyer, was first drawn to Wilberforce by his fierce hatred of slavery, and, when angry, was scarcely controllable. But when Stephen became engaged to his sister, Sally, Wilberforce noted: "Stephen is an improved and improving character, one of those whom religion has transformed and in whom it has triumphed by conquering some natural infirmities." Charles Grant had, on first going to India, lived the conventionally dissolute life of his kind there and soon owed £20,000 as a result of extravagance, gambling and unfortunate business deals. He was converted following the shock of losing his two sons within nine days from fever, and had become "that rare phenomenon in British India at this period, an honest man."

Neither, however, stopped there. Like Wilberforce, they had gone on from this initial experience to face and find the cure for the subtler temptations of political life, such as ambition, rejoicing when an opponent failed or when one outshone a colleague, together with the multitude of prides, hurts and jealousies which often frustrate the best intentions of most political combinations. Among them, St. Paul's recipe for teamwork ("each humbly considering the other the better man") came near to achievement. They learnt from and respected each other, while feeling free to help each other overcome their various defects of character or temperament. Each was pledged not only to the great causes which they undertook together, but also to help their friends attain the character and destiny which God revealed for them.

They talked straight to each other. "Stephen frankly and kindly reproved me," writes Wilberforce on one occasion. "Two of the best friends I have in the world have endeared themselves to me by the same friendly frankness," he tells another who has hesitated to speak his mind. To another friend who wrote supporting Stephen's criticisms, "I thank you for your truly friendly conduct and beg you to join my dear and excellent brother-in-law in helping me correct my infirmities. For this end the first step will always be to tell me my faults." Another Member of Parliament, the future Cardinal Manning's father—not a Clapham intimate, but one of the wider circle—received the same invitation.

James Stephen was particularly blunt. "Your great defect," he wrote to Wilberforce, "has always been want of preparation . . . that you stand so high as you do, is because you could stand much higher if you would, i.e. if you could and would take time to analyze your material." Stephen also criticized the way Wilberforce lavished time on unnecessary correspondence; "Millions will sigh in hopeless wretchedness that Wilberforce's correspondents may not think him unkind or uncivil. Why if you were my Lord Wellington and I Massena, I would undertake to draw off your whole attention from my grand movements, and ruin your army unperceived by teasing your piquets and burning a few cottages on your flanks." His strongest protests were kept for what he believed to be Wilberforce's softness towards Pitt when the latter wearied of well-doing on Abolition. "I still clearly think that you have been improperly silent and that when you see the government loading the bloody altars of commerce . . . you are bound by your situation in which you are placed to cry aloud against it." "Go on, my dear sir, and welcome," replied Wilberforce. "I wish not to abate anything of the force or frankness of your animadversions. . . . Openness is the only foundation and preservative of friendship."

So the men of Clapham sharpened each other. They lived in such intimacy not only because it was necessary but because they enjoyed it. Clapham was often a place for relaxation and delightful time-wasting, as any place where Wilberforce lived was bound to be, in spite of his best resolutions. He would meet one of his friends on the stairs and stand there talking for half an hour, or be drawn off from a "Cabinet Council" to play riotous games with the children. "He was as restless and volatile as a child himself," recalled Thornton's eldest child, Marianne, "and during the long and grave discussions that went on between him and my father and others he was most thankful to refresh himself by throwing a ball or a bunch of flowers at me, or opening the glass door and going off with one for a race on the lawn 'to warm his feet.' One of my first lessons was I must never disturb Papa when he was talking or reading, but no such prohibition existed with Mr. Wilberforce." This could be exasperating. Marianne would hear Dean Milner exclaim on such occasions, "Now, Wilberforce, listen, for no power on earth will make me repeat what I am going to say."

Wives and children took a full part in the Clapham community. Indeed many marriages matured there, for Stephen married Wilberforce's sister, Gisborne Babington's, Charles Eliot Venn's, Babington Macaulay's and Macaulay one of Hannah More's pupils. Wilberforce, at the age of 38, met his own wife on Babington's recommendation.

The children of all these unions grew up together. As the elder Wilberforce children were emerging from babyhood, William Smith's children, including the future mother of Florence Nightingale, had left the schoolroom and the young Macaulays were in the cradle. But the Thorntons, Shores, Grants and the younger Stephens were roughly contemporaries of Wilberforce's children. And mixed in with them were the sons of various Sierra Leone chiefs whom Zachary Macaulay had brought home from Africa with him. At a time when elsewhere in England black boys were usually pages with whom no white boy would mix, there was here complete equality. When the game was soldiers, in fact, the black boys were often designated bandsmen and since bandsmen, in the British Army, flogged defaulters, the black boys "flogged" the white.

Ian Bradley, who lays a good deal of stress on the restrictiveness and dullness of some Victorian Evangelical homes, sees nothing of this kind in the Clapham community; noting that "the Thornton children led blissfully happy lives at their home at Battersea Rise, playing with the Wilberforces and the Macaulays next door." "There was plenty of freedom and good fellowship and reasonable enjoyment for young and old," says Sir George Trevelyan. "There can have been little that was narrow and nothing vulgar in the training that produced Samuel Wilberforce, and Sir James Stephen, and Charles and Robert Grant, and Lord Macaulay."

The children, indeed, grew up naturally in an atmosphere of public affairs. They constantly heard their parents speak of great matters, and Henry Thornton, for example, would discuss his day in Parliament with his daughter, Marianne, from the earliest age. "Wherever she walked," writes E. M. Forster, "the child found herself surrounded by assorted saints. It was not a closed sainthood, there were no entry tests, no esoteric hush-hush. . . ." As soon as she could write legibly she "was made a kind of secretary to my father." A little later she did the family accounts, which "amused me extremely and gave me a pleasant idea of the meaning of the word economy, which he often explained did not mean saving but a right distribution of property."* Later, she wrote to her mother of how this applied to her own spending:

> Mr. T. tells me we must do good both to the bodies and souls of men and to gain an influence over the minds of our equals is perhaps the most necessary, which cannot be done if we are not equally free from austerity and ostentation. Laying this down as a general rule, I am going this morning about my clothes. Moderation and modesty is to be the order of the day, but yet my dress is to be elegant and fashionable.

Beneath everything at Clapham lay a deeper security which transcended all others: an unshaken belief in a future life where family and friends would meet again and would recognize each other and be eternally happy. "Personal immortality today may not be denied by orthodoxy," comments Forster, "but it is played down, it is felt to be self-centred and

---

*Thornton gave away five-sixths of his income before marriage and at least a quarter each year when he had nine children.

anti-social, it is seldom conceived as a change-less background for family life as it was at Battersea Rise."

"It is a travesty which represents the men of Clapham as being made stern and gloomy by an austere religion," adds Howse. "Stern dealing with their own shortcomings did not make them sour towards others. Those who knew them best emphasize an unusual happiness as the striking feature of their family life."

Henry Venn's nephew, John, recalling his own upbringing at Clapham, gives an authentic account of how such happiness was achieved: "These wise men," he wrote, "never endeavoured to mould our unformed opinions into any particular mould. Indeed it was needless for them to preach to us. Their lives spoke far more plainly and convincingly than any words. We saw their patience, cheerfulness, generosity, wisdom and activity daily before us, and we knew and felt that all this was only the natural expression of hearts given to the service of God."

The men of Clapham carried the same qualities into their political lives. Henry Thornton began his Parliamentary career by refusing to pay the customary bribe of a guinea a vote and was re-elected seven times on that basis. Even Babington, with less prestige than Thornton or Wilberforce, remained in Parliament for twenty years without bribery. Wilberforce, it is true, was forced in the 1807 Yorkshire election, when the Fitzwilliam and Lascelles families each spent £100,000 (something like a million and a half in today's currency) to try and unseat him, to allow his committee to "treat" electors in a lesser way, but such was the enthusiasm that only a small sum was required. Meanwhile, in an attempt at permanent reform, he was encouraging Lord Belgrave to bring in a "no-treating" Bill.

In the House of Commons the whole group acted as men who, as one contemporary said, "look to the facts of the case and not to the wishes of the minister, and who before going into the lobby required to be obliged with a reason instead of with a job." Nominally they may have been Tory, like

Wilberforce and Stephen, or Whig like Babington and Smith, and they would normally vote with their parties, but to uphold their principles they would support or oppose any Government—even though their action might be extremely embarrassing to their own party or their friends. The occasions when Wilberforce in great travail of spirit voted against Pitt are the most famous and will be examined later, but it was the same with the others. Thornton voted sometimes with Pitt, sometimes with Fox. "I voted today," he once wrote in his diary after opposing the Government, "as that if my Master had come again at that moment I might have been able to give an account of my stewardship." Wilberforce declared in the early days at Clapham that "it is not in fact talents, in which we are chiefly wanting, but in resolute integrity," and Thornton defined the term as "an honest determination to perform our political duty though the performance should be prejudicial to our general reputation and also to our worldly interest and even though it should endanger our very seat in parliament." In a word, the test for every question was, "Is it morally right?" At the same time they were, as Sir George Trevelyan observed, not crotchety or assertive of artificial scruples, but "the occasions when they made proof of their independence were such as justified, and dignified, their temporary renunciation of their party ties."

Wilberforce was adamant that he would never use his friends' votes—votes which stretched beyond the inner circle to thirty or forty sympathizers at any one time—in order to bribe or coerce the Government, even in the case of Abolition. There were times during both Pitt's and Addington's administrations when this could have been decisive, and some urged him to take advantage of the situation. He always refused. Wheeling and dealing was not his way, and this integrity played its part in gaining for "The Saints" their moral ascendancy in the House. On questions of morality and humanity, as they understood it, they spoke and voted with one voice. And such causes extended far beyond the suppression of the Slave Trade and the reformation of manners. For example, they took the first steps towards humanizing the prisons and the penal code, and pioneered popular education at a time when even a radical like Cobbett thought it "despicable cant and nonsense" and the President of the august Royal Society complained that it would make the labouring classes "fractious and refractory, able to read seditious pamphlets and become insolent to their superiors."

Wilberforce also championed Catholic Emancipation and that of the dissenting sects, and together "The Saints" founded both the Church Missionary Society and the British and Foreign Bible Society. They intervened on behalf of the victims of the Napoleonic Wars, the Greeks then fighting for their freedom, the North American Indians, the Haitians and the Hottentots. Wilberforce too campaigned against the Game Laws, exchanged hot words with Castlereagh about the cruelties of transportation to the penal settlement at Botany Bay in Australia, and opposed flogging in the army.

At home they campaigned against the conditions in which the climbing boys, employed by chimney sweeps, were compelled to work, investigated conditions in the coal mines and were the first, as we shall see, to highlight the need to improve the conditions and shorten the hours of children in the new cotton mills.

Abroad they sought to sustain the struggling colony in Sierre Leone, which they had founded for the accommodation of freed slaves in the 1780s, and worked for a new sense of responsibility in Britain's attitude to India.

Many of these causes were promoted in the teeth of opposition scarcely less violent than that encountered in their principal crusades. Their success was due largely to the quality and persistence of their teamwork, a process in which all their varied talents were employed. Clarkson and Macaulay were the principal researchers; Stephen brought an original mind and passionate hatred of evil, as well as his expert legal knowledge, and he and Macaulay were known as the "authors-general" for all causes. Grant and Shore (later Lord Teignmouth) brought their Indian experience, as well as the influence of their positions. Henry Thornton, the practical banker, planned campaign after campaign, and kept them all on an even keel, while Babington was more and more often the one to whom Wilberforce turned for counsel. Wilberforce himself was the "Agamemnon of the host." He needed them to make him what he was, but they needed him to transform their many interests into a river of reform. His unique position in Parliament and the nation, his genius for friendship, his eloquence and, above all, his faith made him the spearhead of the whole advance.

All of them had their faults, and there were times when, like all closely-knit groups, they showed an unpleasant superiority towards outsiders, as Dean Milner, for one, reminded them. Such occasions however were few and far between, and Coupland's verdict still stands unshaken: "It was, indeed, a unique phenomenon—this brotherhood of Christian politicians. There has never been anything like it since in British public life."

13

The Community in Action

SOME IDEA OF HOW the teamwork of Wilberforce and his friends
worked in practice can be gained by studying the campaign
they waged over the East India Company charter of 1813. The
East India Company at that time controlled British India under
a charter which came up for review by Parliament every
twenty years. In 1793 Wilberforce had put forward two
resolutions, drafted by Grant, empowering the Company to
select and send out fit persons to act as chaplains and
schoolmasters in different parts of India. These had at first
been accepted by the Commons, but then "like a giant roused
from sleep, India House stirred." A special meeting of the
Court of Directors of the Company declared that Wilberforce's
intention was to break up existing institutions by violence and
to force the Christian faith on the natives of India. The House,
alarmed at the commercial implications, threw out Wilberforce's clauses during the Bill's third reading.

The background to this decision was the well-nigh universal view that Britain's relations with India should be purely
commercial and her responsibilities only political. Few be-

113

lieved that the British had any duty to encourage education or even to live morally themselves. It was quite normal for the British in India to have a string of Indian mistresses, and as late as 1810 the Company's *Vade Mecum*, an official booklet for the instruction of young servants of the East India Company, devoted 48 pages to the subject of mistresses, their upkeep, cosmetics and ornaments. It quoted with approval an elderly Englishman who kept sixteen such girls simultaneously and who, on being asked how he looked after them, said: "Oh, I give them a little rice and let them run about."

In these circumstances, it is hardly surprising that opposition to the introduction of Christian missionaries was fierce. Some objected out of regard for India's ancient culture, but most because the presence of missionaries might interfere with business, provoke hostility among Indian soldiers or expose the Englishman's way of life there.

Wilberforce understood little of the mystical or philosophical nature of Hinduism, for this was a period when less was generally known about it. He knew a good deal however about the cruelties which were then involved in it: the burning of widows on their husbands' funeral pyres, human sacrifices and the horrors of the caste system, for example. In any case his conviction that Jesus Christ had come to save all mankind put upon him the imperative duty of opening the way for Christ's ambassadors everywhere. He regarded their exclusion as "next to the slave trade, the foulest blot on the moral character of our country." Grant and Shore, who had first raised the question of missionaries while still in India, were equally scandalized at their exclusion by Parliament, but also felt in Shore's words that Europeans in India "needed to Christianise themselves." So the Clapham brotherhood set to work both in England and in India.

Grant was appointed a Director of the East India Company in 1794, and soon became "the headpiece of the company in Leadenhall Street and its mouthpiece in Parliament." Shore, meanwhile, was persuaded to return to India, Wilberforce having convinced Pitt that he should be appointed

Governor-General. Though by no means a great Governor-General, he set new standards of behaviour. "In a time when to be corrupt was to be like one's neighbour," observed Sir John Kaye, the Victorian Secretary of the India Office and historian of Anglo-India, "he preserved, in privation and poverty, the most inflexible integrity." But even in these great positions Shore and Grant were unable to make much progress in the cause of the missionaries. Shore built a number of churches, and a few chaplains were sent out; but the great Baptist missionary, William Carey, had to take refuge in a Danish enclave. They did however block the demand, following the mutiny of some Indian troops in 1806 which some attributed to "attempts to make them Christians," for all Christian missionaries to be sent home.

The men of Clapham realized that the decisive battle would come in 1813 when the Charter would again come up for review in Parliament. Eighteen months in advance, the "Cabinet Councils" in Clapham began to discuss the campaign. Each man took on a particular responsibility. Gisborne set to work to rouse the clergy. Macaulay began drafting a series of circulars and Babington was set aside as "conspirator-in-chief to organize hundreds of petitions on the pattern first used during the Abolition struggle. Grant prepared his *Observations* which were laid before the Commons, and Shore, back from India as Lord Teignmouth, got ready to give evidence to the Lords. Meanwhile Wilberforce interviewed Perceval, the evangelically minded Prime Minister, and engaged in a series of "political breakfasts" and a "multitude of letters." "In parliamentary measures," he wrote to Hannah More, "more is done out of the House than in it."

Gisborne found that the reaction in religious circles was tepid, and a further setback was in store. On May 11th, 1812, Wilberforce was waiting with Thornton at Babington's house for a working dinner. He was actually praising Perceval's virtue when their host arrived, much agitated, to say that Perceval had been assassinated in the lobby of the House of Commons. No member of the Government which succeeded his could be expected to approach the problem with the same commitment and, when the debate opened in March 1813, the House was indifferent. "The truth is, and a dreadful truth it is," wrote Wilberforce to a friend, "that the opinions of nine-tenths, or at least of a vast majority of the House of Commons, would be against any motion which the friends of religion might make."

So the "Cabinet Councils" became more frequent than ever, even invading the cherished Sunday rest. Wilberforce plunged into a new round of interviews, and a vastly increased campaign for petitions was initiated. Wilberforce wrote personally to each of those who had raised petitions against the Slave Trade. "If every city and town were to petition, the business would acquire a new complexion by the end of May," remarked one of Grant's helpers, Dr. Claudius Buchanan, and so it proved. In June, 1,837 petitions bearing more than half a million signatures were ready, and MPs saw that the country's interest had been militantly engaged.

Ten of the Clapham brotherhood spoke in the debate and when, after wearying days of discussing every aspect of Indian policy and diplomacy, Wilberforce rose to speak, the House was full. "He spoke for three hours, but nobody seemed fatigued," reported Barnes from the Press Gallery. "All indeed were pleased, some with the ingenious artifices of his manner, but most with the glowing language of his heart. Much as I differed from him in opinion, it was impossible not to be delighted with his eloquence . . . He never speaks without exciting a wish that he would say more."

It was an extraordinary performance. In a House which hated sermonizing and was quick to recognize cant, he set out his basic beliefs more fully than perhaps in any other speech. Making full play with the horrors which the debate had revealed, he exclaimed: "The remedy, Sir, is Christianity, which I justly call the appropriate remedy, for Christianity assumes her true character . . . when she takes under her protection those poor degraded beings on whom philosophy looks down with disdain or perhaps with contemptuous condescension. On the very first promulgation of Christianity it was declared by its great Author as 'Glad tidings to the poor,' and, ever faithful to her character, Christianity delights to instruct the ignorant, to succour the needy, to comfort the sorrowful, to visit the forsaken."

He denied that he was advocating compulsory conversion: "Compulsion and Christianity! Why, the very terms are at variance—the ideas are incompatible." He was not asking Parliament to organize Evangelism; he was asking for toleration, "that we should not substantially and in effect prevent others engaging in it."

Lord Erskine, the great advocate, observed that Wilberforce's speech "deserves a place in the library of every man of letters, even if he is an atheist."

The House responded, the Lords let it pass and the East India Company Charter of 1813 guaranteed liberty to the propagation of the Christian faith.

Wilberforce undoubtedly hoped that in the fullness of time the whole of India would be converted to Christianity. He would have been bitterly disappointed by what in fact occurred. Yet Christianity has influenced Indian life at many points. Its stress upon helping others, rather than merely seeking personal perfection, has been demonstrated by countless men and women from Dr. Carey to Mother Teresa.

More immediately, the men of Clapham's victory meant that the British Parliament had for the first time officially recognized that Britain had responsibilities as well as opportunities in India. "If any particular moment marked the change from looting to paternalism, it was the renewal of the East India Company Charter of 1813," comments Furneaux. Paternalism is not a popular word today, but it was a great advance on looting. Nor were Wilberforce and his friends content to drop the matter after their initial victory. They maintained their position in the East India Company's directorate, one of them being Chairman or Deputy Chairman in every year from 1807 to 1830. The fact that their prime interest was in missionary terms had several important consequences. It meant that they were able to stir the interest of the British people in India, because the missionaries' activities captured their imagination just as the anti-slavery campaign had stirred their interest in the state of Africa. "This attitude," writes Bradley, "was to make Britain approach the native races of Africa and Asia with whom it came into contact in the nineteenth century in a way which was different from any other European country. It was also to give the Evangelicals a supreme opportunity to influence national policy in this sphere . . . Their [the Evangelicals'] attitudes provided the inspiration and the basis of Government policy towards India and Africa throughout the first half of the nineteenth century."

The blueprint set out in Grant's *Observations*, originally written in 1792, was more and more adopted. His main aim was to ensure that England's presence in India "shall have been made in our hands, the means, not merely of displaying a government unequalled in India for administrative justice, kindness and moderation, not merely of increasing the security of the subjects and the prosperity of the country, but of advancing social happiness, of ameliorating the moral state of men and of extending a superior light." Lord William Bentinck who was appointed Governor-General in 1828 was a disciple of Grant's and, amongst other things, outlawed thuggee (assassination for religious reasons), suttee (burning of widows alive on their husband's funeral pyres) and female infanticide. In the same way the Charter Act of 1833 was actually drafted by two Claphamites of the second generation, Grant's son Charles and Sir James Stephen, Stephen's son and Wilberforce's nephew. Lord Macaulay's famous educational Minute insisting that teaching in Indian schools shall be in English (another of the main recommendations in Grant's *Observations*) followed two years later. The outstanding example of Clapham principle in action was the Punjab system introduced by Sir Henry Lawrence and his young helpers in the 1840s and 50s.

Similarly, Clapham ideals were for many years dominant in British policy towards Africa. To further this work Sir James Stephen moved to the Colonial Office, where he was Under-

Secretary from 1836 till 1847. His influence was so all-pervasive that he became known as Mr. Mother Country.

The initial victory over the 1813 Charter was won by the methods pioneered in the Abolition fight. John Morley in his *Life of Burke* writes that Burke was right to reject the task of Abolition as beyond his scope. "He was right," Morley comments, "in refusing to hope from political action what could only be effected after the moral preparation of the bulk of the nation—and direct apostleship was not his function." Wilberforce and his friends were better equipped. In fact, where politics is often defined as the "art of the possible," Wilberforce was used by God to make possible today what had been impossible yesterday.

Their methods were followed by generations of reformers. Lord Shaftesbury copied them exactly in his fight to abolish child labour in the factories, a cause he took up in the very year of Wilberforce's death.*

---

*For a short account see my *Brave Men Choose*, pages 87–114.

14

Fisher of Men

WILBERFORCE WAS NEVER MERELY a campaigner, a man of causes. His central desire was that everyone he met should have the chance to discover the same enriching experience which he had been given. This, to him, was the main point of continuing to go into society. Thus he would often spend time before a dinner party thinking out what he called "launchers," topics which would naturally lead on into deeper conversation. Among his papers was found a "Friends' Paper," marked "to be looked at each Sunday," listing thirty of his friends. Against each name stood thoughts of how best to help each to take the next step towards a fully satisfying experience of Christ. His aim was the same, whether the friend was a neighbour's footman, a prisoner under sentence or the Czar of All the Russias.

In the first years after his conversion he suffered some inner conflict between his new piety and his natural gaiety of heart, but Hannah More was once more a sane counsellor. "You are serving God," she wrote, "by making yourself agreeable . . . to worldly but well-disposed people, who would never be attracted to religion by grave and severe divines." His happy ways were an "honest bait" by which acquaintances who were dead and buried in luxury and indulgence could be awakened, for they would realize that he had not been driven to religion for lack of relish for "life." Wilberforce accepted this advice.

Two to be tempted by such "honest bait" were the widowed Countess of Waldegrave and her mother, the Duchess of Gloucester by her second marriage and so a sister-in-law of the King. The King, however, disapproved of her because she was both non-royal by birth and also illegitimate (she was one of the daughters of Horace Walpole's brother by a Pall Mall milliner) and she was therefore cold-shouldered at court. However the change in her became so obvious that even the King relented. Her son, Prince William Frederick, was devoted to Wilberforce and became the one Royal Duke to speak up for Abolition and to work with him on many other causes.

Wilberforce believed in taking every opportunity. Once, late in life, he found himself locked up in a committee room of the House during a division with a man of fashion whom he had not seen for years. The man was obviously embarrassed, but Wilberforce at once said: "You and I, my lord, were pretty well acquainted formerly."

"Alas," came the reply—and then with a deep sigh, "you and I are a great many years older now."

"Yes, we are and for my part I can truly say I do not regret it," said Wilberforce.

"Don't you?" said the other, with what Wilberforce described as "an eager and almost incredulous voice and a look of wondering dejection, which I will never forget."

Even when he studiously avoided religion, people sometimes imagined that he must be talking of it. An old peer was visited by him in his sick bed and Wilberforce spoke of everything except religion. "How are you?" said someone who chanced to come in. "Well enough," said the peer, "considering Wilberforce is sitting here telling me I am going to Hell."

Wilberforce, of course, had many disappointments, but he was nonetheless greatly sought after. The novelist, Fanny Burney, caught his charm in a letter to her father from Sandgate: "Four hours of the best conversation I have ever, nearly enjoyed . . . I had much to communicate, and his drawing me out and comments and episodes were all so judicious, so spirited, so full of information, yet so unassuming, that my shyness all flew away and I felt to be his confidential friend, opening to him upon every occurrence and sentiment with a frankness that is usually won by years of intercourse. I was really and truly delighted and enlightened by him . . . That his discourse should be edifying could not, certainly surprise me; but there was a mixture of simplicity, and vivacity in his manner that I had not expected, and found really captivating." The celebrated Mme. de Stael, coming to London, planned long and with exquisite strategy to get him to dinner with her. Afterwards she said: "I have always heard that he is the most religious, but I now know that he is the wittiest man in England."

Even an old reprobate like the Prince Regent treated him with respectful affection. When after the battle of Waterloo, the Prussian Marshal Blucher sent his aide-de-camp to report to the Prince Regent, the Prussian representative said he had orders to report to one other person in England, Mr. Wilberforce. The Prince replied, "Go to him yourself then by all means, you will be delighted with him." Later that year, Wilberforce being in Brighton, the Prince pressed him to come to dinner. He reminded him of the first time they had met, when Wilberforce had sung at the Duchess of Devonshire's ball in 1782. "All unawares," related Coupland, "the Prince had provided Wilberforce with a 'launcher' and the result was delightful. 'We are both, I trust, much altered since, Sir,' was Wilberforce's startling reply. The Prince took a strong hold on himself. 'Yes,' he responded with somewhat laboured gravity, 'the time which has gone by must have made a great alteration in us.' 'Something better than that, too, I trust, Sir.' Even now the Prince was not deterred. He repeated his invitation to

dinner and assured Wilberforce, with engaging candour, that
'he should hear nothing in his house to give him pain.' And so
it was both on that occasion and at another dinner party later
on." Indeed, when the Prince discovered that it was inconvenient for Wilberforce to visit the Pavilion so often, he asked
him "in the handsomest way possible" to suit himself and just
come when he wished.

Many are astonished that a man of Wilberforce's principles was so sought after in those loose Regency days (the
Prince Regent, later George IV, was at the centre of the moral
laxity). A contemporary writes that "every face lit up with
pleasure at his entry" when he came late to a big dinner.
Perhaps some of Wilberforce's secret lay in his being so
crystal-clear and unself-conscious about his principles. Being
free from worry about himself, he was free to think of others.

Not everyone, however, was so grateful for his attentions.
In his later years a senior civil servant from the Colonial Office,
whom he had felt bound to pursue somewhat relentlessly,
remarked: "It is the fashion to speak of Wilberforce as a gentle,
yielding character, but I can only say that he is the most
obstinate, impracticable fellow with whom I ever had to do."
Coming away from a Minister who had appointed a man of
notoriously immoral character to high office abroad, Wilberforce said, "I conceived that the honour of the country was
involved, and therefore I plainly told him my mind, and that he
would have to answer hereafter for his choice, but he was so
angry that I thought he would have knocked me down."

There was, on the other hand, no touch of superiority
about him. As Coupland says, "His moral standards were not,
so to speak, of his own prescription. A revelation had come to
him, without any conscious volition on his part, and in the light
of it he was bound to live as he did. To any of the others, any
day, he believed, the same call might come with the same
results . . . He could refuse to conform without seeming to
condemn—a rare gift."

As may well be imagined, the person whom—next to his
own children—Wilberforce most desired to see a "true Chris-

tian" was Pitt. Winston Churchill sees this as a contest between Wilberforce and Pitt's other close associate, Henry Dundas. In the centre he pictures "the grave, precocious young statesman, eloquent, incorruptible and hardworking." On one side is Dundas, "a good-humoured, easy-going materialist, embodying the eighteenth century with its buying of seats, its full-blooded enjoyment of office, its secret influences and its polished scepticism"; on the other, Wilberforce who, he says, "became the keeper of the young minister's conscience," holding him not unsuccessfully to higher ways and, when he seemed tardy, "never permitting a syllable of doubt to be spoken unchallenged about his friend." Pitt regarded himself as dependent on the votes and interests for which Dundas stood and continually compromised with them. Cataloguing the failure of so many of Pitt's policies, Churchill concludes: "Pitt had been overcome by the dead hand of the eighteenth century." Wilberforce commented, "For personal purity, disinterestedness, integrity and love of country I have never known his equal." But, for himself alone in his journal, he added: "The truth is that, great man as he was, he had very little insight into human nature."

Wilberforce did not see himself as the "keeper of Pitt's conscience." His anxious concern, rather, was to keep his own. He strove, often with anguish, to decide his attitude to every question by the light that God gave him. Although he found that he could back Pitt far more often than he had at first feared, he sometimes had to oppose him, often at highly inconvenient moments. These occasions caused him much pain: "I am grieved to the heart, fearful I must differ," he notes when one such issue arose.

As the 1794–5 crisis over Pitt's war policy loomed, he wrote to Edward Eliot, "I need hardly say that the prospect of a public difference with Pitt is extremely painful to me, and, though I trust his friendship for me has sunk too deep in his heart to be soon worn out, I confess it hangs on me like a weight I cannot remove when I anticipate the whole situation. My spirits are hardly equal to the encounter. However I hope it will please God to enable me to act the part of an honest man on this trying occasion. . . ." Indeed the difference was sharp. Wilberforce felt compelled to speak out for another attempt at peace with France and was, for a time, one of the most unpopular men in England, accused of treachery by the Tories and of halfheartedness by the Whigs. Windham called him "a wicked little fanatical imp" and even Dean Milner took him to task as unpatriotic. More important to Wilberforce, "Pitt," in the Duke of Portland's words, "seemed pretty seriously hurt by it." The gap yawned for some months, and was widened soon after by Pitt's "fury" when his friend intervened successfully against granting the full £125,000 to meet the Prince of Wales' debts. But in the end Pitt moved round to Wilberforce's view on the war and there was a merry party in Eliot's garden at Broomfield "walking, foining, laughing and reading verses as before." Again in 1797 Wilberforce felt compelled, privately and then publicly, to warn the Government against financial dishonesty and extravagance and he notes in his diary: "Saw little of Pitt this last week— vexed him by plain dealing."

There was a clash on a more personal matter when Wilberforce heard that Pitt had fought a duel with another MP, George Tierney. Horrified, Wilberforce hurried to London and put down a motion against duelling. "Your motion is one for my removal," Pitt wrote him angrily, and after some days, Wilberforce, seeing that Pitt's premiership and not duelling would be the point voted upon, withdrew the motion.

Pitt's mute appeal to his old friend during the debate in 1805 on the corruption that Dundas, now Lord Melville, had allowed to develop at the Admiralty was less successful. "It required no little effort to resist the fascination of that penetrating eye," commented Wilberforce later, but he did resist and his speech was the decisive word which drove Melville into retirement.* Some say this event so weakened Pitt's Cabinet

*Wilberforce, however, refused to join in the hunt and impeachment of Melville.

that it hastened his death and it is hard to agree with Wilberforce that his action had no part in it. Pitt, however, never reproached Wilberforce for it because he knew that Wilberforce could do no other. Indeed their natural affection flowed deeper in the last months of Pitt's life than for some time.

These occasions of divergence, no less than the more numerous times of consultation and agreement, had a great influence upon Pitt. Wilberforce's sons reported the common view that only two public events ever caused Pitt to lose sleep: the Naval mutiny at the Nore and Wilberforce's opposition in 1794. Be that as it may, Pitt knew that prudence, no less than friendship, made it advisable for him to match his measures, where possible, to Wilberforce's conscience and so carry with him that powerful independent voice.

Furneaux puts the other side of the story:

> Wilberforce was constantly soliciting Pitt's help for his various causes, few of which were concerned with the mainstream of politics. Pitt's patience and understanding were extraordinary. He would oblige Wilberforce whenever possible and would listen to his demands, however outrageous, without ever asking for any *quid pro quo*. Wilberforce's conscience was an inconvenient and sometimes destructive factor in politics. He might present a motion in the Commons against duelling when Pitt himself had just fought a duel. He might oppose a war in which the country was struggling for its existence. He might demand that the militia should cease drilling on Sundays when Napoleon's army was massed in Boulogne. He might deprive the Government of its most valuable Minister at the most critical moment of the war. But Pitt never protest-

---

"Must I join the triumph over a fallen friend?" he exclaimed to one who urged him to do so. Melville may have felt this objectivity, for the next time they met, years later in a narrow passage between Horse Guards and Downing Street, he greeted Wilberforce warmly. "I would have given a thousand pounds for that handshake," noted Wilberforce.

ed. Wilberforce admired him more than any other man in the world, a lack of religious principles being the only flaw he could perceive in Pitt's character. He was as great and as good as a man without religion could be.

Yes, Pitt's patience was amazing, but is Furneaux quite fair to Wilberforce? Do his instances show Wilberforce as a "sometimes destructive factor?"

Wilberforce withdrew the motion on duelling as soon as he had made his general point and saw the threat it posed to Pitt and stable government.

His protest against the militia training on a Sunday, incredible as it may seem today, was all of a piece with his deepest convictions. Steeped in the Old as well as the New Testament, he believed that the defence of a nation depended at least as much on obeying God's commandments as on military preparations, which, incidentally, he supported energetically in every other way.

The more serious charge—that Wilberforce deprived Pitt of Lord Melville, then First Lord of the Admiralty, at the most critical moment of the war—is eased when one remembers that this was a matter of corruption, about which Lord Melville had lied to Pitt and the House. His resignation set a pattern for ministerial conduct approved and observed even to this day. There was, also, at least as good a man available to fill his place. Melville's cousin, Admiral Sir Charles Middleton, who, on Melville's own recommendation, became First Lord, was more fitted than any civilian to direct the sea campaign which led up to the victory over French sea power in the decisive battle of Trafalgar. "It is doubtful," comments Pollock, "whether Melville or any landsman, or even St. Vincent, would have reacted fast enough to the exceptional circumstances of 1805: or found such instant rapport with Nelson when the Commander-in-Chief and the First Lord met briefly at last."

None of this lessens one's admiration for Pitt's patience or one's sympathy for his dilemmas. Men of Wilberforce's robust conscience are often awkward to work with, but they are not necessarily less practical than pragmatists of the Melville stamp.

Furneaux is, of course, right in saying that Wilberforce had dreamed of something greater than influencing Pitt in this way. He had hoped to implant a self-propagating faith in his friend. Thus, in the final sketch of Pitt which he wrote in 1822, he returned to his respect and admiration for his friend, and to his regret that Pitt had not resolved at the outset of his career "to govern the country by principle rather than by influence." From such a resolve, he wrote, tremendous consequences would have flowed. The whole body politic would have been cleansed and strengthened, and even such a cataclysm as the French revolution would have left it unshaken.

"Such a spirit of patriotism would have been kindled, such a generous confidence in the King's Government would have been diffused throughout all classes," continued Wilberforce, "that the very idea of the danger of our being infected with the principles of French licentiousness . . . would have been an apprehension not to be admitted within the bosom of the most timid politician; while the various reforms which would have taken place and the manifest independence of Parliament would have generated and ensured in the minds of all reasonable men a continually increased gratitude and affection for the constitution and laws of the land. On the other hand the French . . . could never have been so blind to their manifest interest as to engage their people in war with Great Britain from any idea of our confederating with the Crowned Heads of Europe to crush the rising spirit of liberty in France."

Wilberforce believed that had Pitt made the attempt to "govern by principle" from the start, he would have succeeded. "No one who had not been an eye-witness could conceive the ascendancy which Mr. Pitt then possessed over the House of Commons," he wrote. "All his faculties then possessed the bloom of youthful beauty as well as the full vigour of maturer age. His mind was ardent, his principles pure, his patriotism warm, his mind as yet unsullied by habitually associating with men of worldly ways of thinking and acting, in short with a class that may not be unfitly termed 'trading politicians.'" Yet something more would be needed, "something," in Coupland's summary, "in the nature of a miracle, something, at any rate, beyond the unaided power of man." It was this greater experience which Wilberforce always coveted for his friend, an experience which would enable him to be not just a bold reformer, but a statesman who strove to be controlled by God. Again and again Wilberforce's imagination takes fire as he considers the effect of such a liberation. "Who can say what would have been the effect of those moral and spiritual secretions which throughout the whole political body would have gradually produced their blessed effects?"

Here, Furneaux objects, Wilberforce's final estimate of his friend, was "at least part wishful thinking." "Pitt, as Prime Minister, had to manipulate the delicate machinery of influence so as to provide a continuous and constructive Government. Wilberforce never fully understood this side of politics. To him 'influence' like 'party' was bad, although he was prepared, on occasion, to use it himself. . . ."

It is only fair to note that Wilberforce himself gave up "influence" in the technical eighteenth-century sense (the politician's use of "interest" to secure Government favour for friends and relations) in 1794. Writing to Pitt on September 6th of that year, he had referred to "the last case of patronage about which I will ever worry you," and he kept to this resolution, in spite of his mother's annoyance that he would not push forward his brother or several poorer relations. He still suggested candidates for church preferment (most of whom were turned down through the influence of Bishop Pretyman) and sometimes asked Pitt to find a place for someone who had suffered in the West Indies for his advocacy of Abolition. He, however, refused any longer—it had taken him eight years to identify the practice as corrupt—to further his electoral chances by soliciting favours for his constituents. "This was a hard sacrifice," as he wrote twenty years later, "but duty required it."

Whether, in fact, Pitt as Prime Minister could have done the same is much more doubtful. His Government, as Furneaux points out, was sustained, especially at the beginning, by an amazing combination of interests, few of which were over-loyal to him as a person. "The dead hand of the eighteenth century," in Churchill's phrase, was a reality and it was no disgrace to be "overcome" by it. Still, it was no bad thing for Wilberforce to have so high a vision for his friend, particularly as he himself did so much to change the situation as the years went by.

For as Wilberforce looked at Parliament with new eyes, following his conversion, he was appalled to see that most MPs regarded it as a stadium for place-seeking and faction fighting rather than a serious assembly for settling the nation's affairs. It was, he said, "degraded by the languor with which the public interest is treated compared with the animation called forth by petty party and personal struggles." He believed it should be "the moral mint of the nation in which moral and political principles receive their stamp and currency."

When he began, he was one of only three members vaguely identified with "vital Christianity." In the next fifty years before the Reform Bill, over a hundred Members sat in the House who thought as he did and an equal number were active in the House of Lords. Their presence did much to transform the House from a club mainly concerned with the interests of its Members to an assembly responsible for the public good. He and his friends introduced wider issues and established that they ought to be decided, not by narrow self-interest, but by moral right. The public who during the age of Fox had begun to hold all politicians in contempt, responded, and during the succeeding century statesmen, to be successful, were compelled to live, or at least pretend to live, morally and for the public good. This, as Wilberforce had foreseen, increased the amount of hypocrisy shown by some politicians, but more importantly it established politics as an honourable profession for honest men.

For Pitt, of course, Wilberforce's great wish was simple—

that he should add to his great human qualities the added stimulus of a personal experience of Christ. It was with this in mind that he often sought to continue that "serious talk" begun in 1784. In 1792 he went down to Walmer with this in mind, failed the first day and was much distressed. "At night alone with Pitt, but talked only politics—did not find myself equal to better talk—O Christ help me." Next day he did better. "Had a serious talk with Pitt—interrupted, or should have had more." At the time of Pitt's death he adds in sadness, "I have a thousand times wished and hoped that a quiet interval would be afforded him, perhaps in the evening of his life, in which he and I might confer freely on the most important of all subjects. But the scene is closed—for ever."

It was, it seemed to Wilberforce, often Bishop Pretyman who barred the way. Pretyman was a complacent High Anglican, whose dislike of what Wilberforce stood for was only fully revealed in 1900 when the Bishop almost succeeded in getting Pitt to tighten the Toleration Act so as to deny licences to preach both to many dissenting preachers and to many of those Anglican clergy whom Wilberforce respected most. On that occasion, Wilberforce spoke personally to Pitt about it. "I confess," he wrote afterwards, "I never till then knew how deep a prejudice his mind had conceived against the class of clergy to whom he knew me to be attached . . . his language was such as to imply that he thought ill of their moral character, and it clearly appeared that the prejudice arose out of the confidence he reposed in the Bishop of Lincoln."

So, as Pitt lay dying, Wilberforce remained restless at Broomfield, longing to go to his friend, but aware that Bishop Pretyman was keeping the ministrations in his own hands. "I never could forgive his never proposing prayer to our poor old friend Pitt . . . till within about six hours before his dissolution," he wrote to Bankes twenty-five years later.

15

"The Practical View"

IT WAS LARGELY IN the hope of reaching Pitt and others of his friends—some of whom had strange ideas of what he really thought—that Wilberforce wrote his book: *A Practical View of the Prevailing Religious System of Professed Christians in the Higher and Middle Classes in this Country Contrasted with Real Christianity.*

It had been a long time in the planning. As far back as 1789 he had considered writing such a book, but rejected the idea in case "the dread of an over-righteous man would deter people" (and especially "P and other great men, even G himself"*) from cooperating with him for national reform.

By 1793, however, when he first began to write, his commitment was so well-known and his two great causes in such a state—Abolition becalmed and the reformation of manners well launched—that the situation had changed. Owing to his many other concerns, however, it was not until

---

*Pitt and George III.

1797 that he took the finished manuscript to Thomas Cadell, the publisher of Johnson's *Lives of the Poets*. Cadell was not optimistic. A religious book by a politician was unheard of, and would not sell. However, on finding that Wilberforce intended to sign the book, he allowed: "I think we may venture on 500 copies." What he lacked in enthusiasm, he made up for in speed, producing the book with its 491 pages, plus index, in two months.

The effect was extraordinary. "It was read at the same moment, by all the leading persons in the nation. An electric shock could not be felt more vividly and instantaneously," wrote one observer. "Everyone talked about it . . . It was acknowledged that such an important book had not appeared for a century." It immediately became—and remained for fifty years—a best seller. Five editions and 7,500 copies were sold in six months, and by 1826 fifteen editions had been printed in England and twenty-five in America, and it had been translated into French, Italian, Spanish, Dutch and German. Coupland judged it "one of the outstanding achievements of Wilberforce's life" and Philip Anthony Brown, in his *The French Revolution in English History*, a work edited by J. L. Hammond in 1918, says it marked the beginning of the influence of Evangelicalism on the upper classes.

Wilberforce sent an early copy to Pitt with the relevant passages (parts of chapters four and six) marked in the margin. What Pitt thought of it we do not know, but Burke spent much of the last two days of his life reading it. He spoke of the "unspeakable comfort" it brought him. "If I live, I shall thank Wilberforce for having sent such a book into the world," he said to Mrs. Crewe. Thornton noted that "the bishops in general approve, though some more warmly, some more coldly." "Many of Wilberforce's gay* friends admire it. His political friends, and some gay ones, also do but dip and find

*He wrote, of course, before the current corruption of the word.

no fault. Several have recognised the likeness of themselves
. . ." he added.

A backhanded kind of tribute, which Byron enjoyed
relating, came from Sheridan, never much of a Wilberforce-
admirer. At about this time, he was found in the street by a
watchman "fuddled, bewildered and almost insensible."

"Who are you, Sir?" said the watchman. No answer.

"What's your name?"—a hiccup.

"What's your name?" persisted the watchman.

When the answer at length came, it was solemn and
impressive: "Wilberforsssh."

With others, the book went deeper. A libertine, formerly
a devotee of Voltaire, wrote that the book had reformed him,
while an anonymous correspondent said he had bought a
small freehold in Yorkshire so that he might, by his vote, offer
a small tribute of respect.

The book went on bearing fruit through its readers. Arthur
Young, the eminent agriculturalist, began reading it with
indifference, but it "made such an impression that I scarcely
knew how to lay it aside. It excited a very insufficient degree of
repentance and an even more insufficient view of my interest
in the Great Physician of souls." He and Wilberforce became
friends and worked together on many projects for the better
feeding of the poor. Young also made an attempt to pass on
his new experience to his patron, the Duke of Grafton, a
former Prime Minister.

Legh Richmond was another who was to spread its
message. While he was a somewhat worldly curate in the Isle
of Wight, he read Wilberforce's book far into the night and, for
the first time, "understood the vital character of personal
religion, the corruption of the human heart and the way of
salvation through Jesus Christ." He was destined to become a
kind of successor to Hannah More in the writing of moral tales
and sold some five million copies of them in his lifetime.

The effect of *A Practical View* was certainly not due to its
literary style, for it shows little of the vivaciousness of Wilberforce's speech or even of his letters. Its very discursiveness

may have been attractive after the dense theological writing of the times and the charity of his severest criticisms a refreshing contrast to the furious name-calling of current religious controversy. The secret of its success, apart from its obvious sincerity, may have been that it was written by a national figure at a time of national crisis—the Bank of England having suspended payments shortly before it appeared and the Mutiny at the Nore taking place just afterwards.

Wilberforce's compendious title, which reads so strangely in this age of slogans, was an exact description of the book's contents. Although it did, as we have seen, reach the wholly irreligious, its main object was:

> Not to convince the sceptic or to answer the arguments of persons who avowedly oppose the fundamental doctrines of our religion; but to point out the scanty and erroneous system of the bulk of those who belong to the class of orthodox Christians, and to contrast their defective scheme with a representation of what the author apprehends to be real Christianity.

As his title foreshadowed, Wilberforce's approach was practical. He emphasized that it was not enough to profess Christianity, to go to church on Sundays and to live a decent life, but that Christianity must be allowed to pervade and penetrate every corner of a Christian's existence. Besides passionately setting forth the fundamentals of the Christian faith and experience, it contained his views on how religion should affect the rich, the poor and the statesman, as well as giving his own vision of the Utopia which the world could become.

Stressing the next world as firmly as the present, he stated what to him had become the clearest of facts, that "this present scene, with all its cares and all its gaieties, will soon be rolled away" and that we must "stand before the judgement seat of Christ." Nothing was sadder than society's "utter forgetfulness of its being the great business of life to secure our admission into Heaven and to prepare our hearts for its service and enjoyments."

The true Christian, Wilberforce insisted, recognizes that the doctrine of grace is "the cardinal point on which the whole of Christianity turns"; that only by "an absolute surrender of soul and body to the will and service of God" can he hope for salvation; that every purpose he has in his life must be tested by the pattern of the life of Christ.

Coming to the chapter headed "A brief enquiry into the present state of Christianity in this country . . . and its importance to us as a political community," Wilberforce stated that true religion has been steadily declining in England. The growth of prosperity, the splendour and luxury of London and the prevalence—"much as we are indebted to it"—of the commercial spirit had led to the "discontinuance of the religious habits of a purer age." Christianity is "scarcely at all the object of study" of the bulk of nominal Christians, to be lukewarm was a step towards unbelief and the tone of literature was already sceptical. "The time is fast approaching when Christianity will be almost as openly disavowed in the language, as in fact it has already supposed to have disappeared from the conduct of men, when infidelity will be held to be the necessary appendage of a man of fashion and to believe will be deemed to be the indication of a feeble mind." If anyone doubted that, let him look at France.

Against this picture he set that of his ideal community where everyone leads a Christian life:

> If any country were indeed filled with men, each thus dili-
> gently discharging the duties of his own station without
> breaking in upon the rights of others, but on the contrary
> endeavouring, so far as he might be able, to forward their
> views and promote their happiness—all would be active and
> harmonious in the goodly frame of human society. There
> would be no jarrings, no discord. The whole machine of civil
> life would work without obstruction or disorder and the

course of its movements would be like the harmony of the spheres.

For Christianity's supreme political value is its direct hostility to selfishness—"the moral distemper of political communities," the cause wherever it appears, among governors or governed, rich or poor, of political disorder and decay.

In whatever class or order of society Christianity prevails, she sets herself to counteract the particular mode of selfishness to which that class is liable. Affluence she teaches to be liberal and beneficent; authority to bear its faculties with meekness and to consider the various cares and obligations belonging to its elevated station as being conditions on which that station is conferred. Thus, softening the glare of wealth and moderating the insolence of power, she renders the inequalities of the social state less galling to the lower orders, whom she instructs, in their turn, to be diligent, humble, patient: reminding them that their more lowly path has been allotted to them by the hand of God; that it is their part faithfully to discharge its duties, and contentedly to bear its inconveniences; that the present state of things is very short . . . that the peace of mind which religion offers indiscriminately to all ranks affords more true satisfaction than all the expensive pleasures which are beyond the poor man's reach; that in this view the poor have the advantage; that if their superiors enjoy more abundant comforts, they are also exposed to many temptations from which the inferior classes are happily exempted; that, "having food and raiment, they should be therewith content," since their situation in life, with all its evils, is better than they have deserved at the hand of God; and finally that all human distinctions will soon be done away, and the true followers of Christ will all, as children of the same Father, be alike admitted to the possession of the same Heavenly inheritance.

A hundred years later, J.L. and Barbara Hammond in

The Town Labourer were to pick out this passage about the poor, which, in the eyes of a twentieth-century reader, would seem to leave them at the mercy of the rich for ever. In particular, the Hammonds fasten upon the statement, which reads heartlessly to any modern reader, that the life of the poor "with all its evils, is better than they have deserved at the hand of God." Standing by itself this does indeed read not merely paternalistically (and the best of that age was paternalist rather than socialist) but callously. To an eighteenth-century reader, however, as Pollock points out, it was simply an application of Article IX of the Thirty-Nine Articles of the Church of England: that in "every person born into this world" whether rich or poor, the corruption of the flesh wrought by Original Sin "deserveth God's wrath and damnation." And to most contemporary readers, too, misunderstandings would be lessened by the knowledge that the author had, above all public men of the day, proved himself the friend of the poor and had challenged the rich to care for them.

Wilberforce wrote against the background of the revolution of atheism and blood in France, where a whore had been seated in state on the Altar of Notre Dame: and at a moment of crisis in the war with that country. He looked for "an antidote to the malignity of venom which is storing up in another country," but he came back again and again to the need for change in Britain itself. He concluded:

> It would be an instance in myself of that very false shame which I have condemned in others, if I were not boldly to avow my firm persuasion that to the decline of Religion and Morality our national difficulties must, both directly and indirectly, be chiefly ascribed; and that my only solid hopes for the well-being of my Country depend, not so much on her fleets and armies, not so much on the wisdom of her rulers or the spirit of her people, as on the persuasion that she still contains many who love and obey the Gospel of Christ; that their intercessions may yet prevail; that, for the sake of these, Heaven may still look upon us with an eye of favour.

Another event of major importance was to befall Wilberforce in the months after the book appeared. For in April 1797 he was to meet and marry Barbara Spooner.

16

Domestic Life of a Reformer

THE DOMESTIC LIFE OF a reformer—or, indeed, of any public man—does not always run smoothly. Special pressures are imposed upon him and his family. Sometimes those pressures break up a marriage or result in the reformer's work being slowed down or even brought to a standstill. Charles Wesley virtually ceased his itinerant ministry after marrying Sally Gwynne and settling down in his domestic cocoon in Bristol. John was of sterner stuff. When his true love, to whom he regarded himself as engaged, was married almost by conspiracy, as he felt, to a colleague and he rebounded into the arms of the utterly unsuitable Mrs. Vazeille, he cheerfully let his wife drag him across the room by his hair, but never for a moment relaxed his mission. "No trap so mischievous to the field preacher as wedlock," commented their friend Berridge upon the Wesleys' and George Whitefield's marriages. "Matrimony has quite maimed Charles and might have spoiled John and George if a wise Master had not graciously sent them a brace of ferrets."

The future Lord Shaftesbury, on the other hand, reached

into one of the most profligate families in the kingdom to find his Min. She was his spirited and devoted partner for forty-two years of enormous effort, won most of her family, including her stepfather Lord Palmerston, to his side and died with the words "None but Christ" on her lips.

Wilberforce's charm and good nature had always made him attractive to women, but his name was never linked with one until at the age of thirty-eight he suddenly married twenty-year-old Barbara Spooner. Many a woman had cast longing eyes towards him, including, it would seem, Dorothy Wordsworth, who considered him "one of the best of men." In 1790 she protested that he would "look for a lady of many more accomplishments than I can boast, and besides he is as unlikely as any man ever to marry at all as any man I know."

In fact, unknown to Dorothy, Wilberforce had been in love that winter, perhaps for the first time. The girl was a Miss H, probably a niece of Henry Addington*, and Wilberforce was brokenhearted when she became engaged to someone else while he hesitated. The fact was that Wilberforce, while deeply affected, had sensed an incompatibility between them, "a difference in views and Plans of Life." To hold back was hard for his warm nature, and the whole episode taught him "that when Love comes into question, or even an approximation to it, I should find it very difficult if not impossible to preserve that composure which I have found nothing else so efficacious in disturbing." Sexual passion, he recognized, could be strong enough to sway him from his faith and purpose.

Thereafter, he often said that he "doubted if he would ever change his situation." "The state of public affairs concurs with other causes in making me feel I must finish my journey alone," he wrote. "Then consider how extremely I am occupied. What should I have done had I been a family man for the

---

*Then Speaker of the House. He later became Prime Minister and, as Lord Sidmouth, prominent in many administrations.

last three weeks, worried from morning till night? But I must not think of such matters now, it makes me feel my solitary state too sensibly."

He wrote that letter in the winter of 1796, six months after Henry Thornton married Wilberforce's friend since childhood, Marianne Sykes—an event which transformed Wilberforce from a full partner at Battersea Rise into a welcome guest. That fact, combined with the happiness which he perceived in the Thorntons, resulted in his speaking of marriage to Babington at Bath the following spring. Babington felt he knew exactly the person: Barbara Spooner, the beautiful daughter of a Birmingham merchant and banker;* and, by what can hardly have been a total coincidence, Wilberforce received a letter from her almost at once asking his spiritual counsel. Wilberforce took this as providential, and a whirlwind courtship ensued. He received her letter on April 13th, met her on the 15th and by the 23rd, to Babington's alarm (and ignoring Milner's pleas to delay) had proposed and been accepted. Babington need not have worried. Wilberforce had fallen head-over-heels in love and was to stay that way all his life. Others doubted his choice, but he always numbered "a domestic happiness beyond what could have been conceived possible" the chief among his blessings.

They were married in Bath on May 30th and spent most of their short honeymoon with Hannah More and her sisters at Cheddar. Hannah pronounced the bride "a pretty, pleasing pious woman" and "had never seen a poor honest gentleman more desperately in love" than the bridegroom. Wilberforce himself wrote to Montague that his dearest Barbara's mind was disposed exactly as he would wish. "She wishes to retire as much as possible from the giddy crowd and to employ herself

---

*"Her fortune (£5,000) small and the family not by any means grand," said Thornton. Duncombe, Wilberforce's fellow Member for Yorkshire, wrote to him: "You will perhaps judge my way of thinking old fashioned and queer, but I am greatly pleased that you have not chosen your partner from among the titled fair ones of the land."

in 'keeping her own heart' and in promoting the happiness of her fellow creatures. I really did not think there was such a woman. There seems to be an entire coincidence in our intimacy and interests and pursuits."

Time was to throw some doubt on that "entire coincidence," but he himself seemed hardly to notice it. He rejoiced that she was not a "political hostess" nor a "pavilion-mongering woman" and simply loved her as she was. Marianne Thornton, when asked if he had not married the wrong woman, later said that if he had not been married to Barbara "no one would have known how much of an angel was in him if they had not seen his behaviour to one whose tastes must have tried his patience so much." He showed no signs of being conscious of such a martyrdom.

To the objective eye, Barbara would certainly seem to have had her drawbacks. Marianne's daughter, another Marianne, no doubt reflected her mother's view as well as her own in her longer sketch:

She [Barbara] was extremely handsome and in some ways very clever, but very deficient in common sense, a woman with narrow views and selfish aims, that is if selfishness can be so called when it took the form of idolatry of her husband, and thinking everything in the world ought to give way to what she thought expedient for him. Instead of helping him forward in the great works which it appeared Providence had given him to do, she always considered she was hardly used when he left her side, and instead of making his home attractive to the crowds of superior people that he invited, her love of economy made her anything but a hospitable hostess. Yet the oddity and queerness of the scenes that went on there often made up, especially to young people, for all other deficiencies.

Neither Marianne really liked Barbara, and both adored Wilberforce; so there was probably exaggeration here. The writer, too, did not know Barbara until after her near-fatal illness, which greatly increased her nervousness. Dorothy Wordsworth admired her "goodness and patience and motherliness," but objected to her "slowness and whineiness of manner."

Barbara in fact was a kindly soul who tried hard to be a companion to her husband and to share her children's enthusiasms, but she was a fusser. She fussed about Wilberforce's health and his many engagements, and finally worried herself into an ill-health which hampered his public life. She also fussed about money and about everything to do with the children. Like her husband she believed that a parent's first responsibility was to foster the children's spiritual welfare, and neither would end a letter without a good ration of spiritual advice or sentiment. But whereas Wilberforce was always cheerful, she would easily fall into gloom or shrill despair. Nevertheless her children appreciated her—"never was there a tenderer mother, rarely one more sensible or more able," said Samuel—and her over-protectiveness of her husband may have prolonged his life. To please her, he dined out much less (poor cousin Carrington declared his "non-Methodist friends" never saw him because of her), and this may have conserved his energies.

She was a poor housekeeper. The kind of oddity to which Marianne Thornton referred was a breakfast, attended as usual by "the most extraordinary mixture of guests," bidden and unbidden, including Dean Milner of Carlisle:

> To use a Yorkshire expression of his [Wilberforce's]—Everyone was expected to fend for themselves. He was so shortsighted he could see nothing beyond his own plate, which Mrs. W took care to supply with all he wanted till the Dean's stentorian voice was heard roaring "There is nothing on earth to eat," and desiring the servants to bring some bread and butter, he would add "and bring plenty without limit," while Mr. W would join in with "thank you, thank you kindly Milner, for seeing to these things, Mrs. W is not strong enough to meddle much in domestic matters."

Broomhill, which Wilberforce bought from Edward Eliot's executors after his much lamented death in late 1797, was their first home. It was an odd community by Thornton standards. There might be no hedges between the properties, but there was no doubt where Wilberforce's rough shrubberies ended and Thornton's trim lawns began. Wilberforce had thirteen or fourteen servants, about the average for his rank, but he tended to hire them for anything but their efficiency, and never turned the useless or the infirm away. They adored him and ran the place atrociously, without his worrying or Barbara's seeming to notice. The old coachman Thomas drove like a madman when either in drink or passion. From time to time Wilberforce decided to dismiss him, but never did. It was this man of whom Wilberforce spoke when he met with bad temper in a friend's housekeeper. "You know the Indians have a way of getting oddly contrasted animals to fight each other," he mused. "I really long to set our old coachman and this fine lady in single combat." On another occasion, Marianne noted: "Things go in the old way, the house thronged with servants who are all lame or impotent or blind, or kept from charity, an ex-secretary kept because he is grateful, and his wife because she nursed poor Barbara, and an old butler who they wish would not stay but then he is so attached, and his wife who was a cook but now she is so infirm. All this is rather as it should be however for one rather likes to see him so completely in character and would willingly despair of getting one's plate changed at dinner and hear a chorus of Bells all day which nobody answers for the sake of seeing Mr. Wilberforce in his element."

All attended family prayers twice a day, each kneeling against a chair, with Wilberforce in the middle kneeling against a table. Such prayers, which Wilberforce had first started in Wimbledon in November 1785, lasted ten minutes, and Wilberforce liked them to be cheerful. He was imitated in thousands of households throughout Britain.

Breakfast was generally at about ten and was one of the great occasions of the day. People came for the brilliant and varied table-talk, which was sometimes a grave discussion on Abolition or other issues of the day, but could as easily, as James Stephen relates, be "a sort of galvanic stream of vivacity, humour and warm-heartedness" from Wilberforce, covering an amazing range of subjects. As James Stephen's son notes, "Being himself amused and interested by everything, whatever he said became amusing and interesting . . . His presence was as fatal to dullness as to immorality. His mirth was irresistible as the first laughter of childhood." The stream of people who thronged to him—Hannah More used to say he lived in "such domestic retirement that he does not see above three and thirty people at breakfast"—made the Wilberforces live in "a kind of domestic publicity," which cannot have been easy for so family-centred a woman as Barbara. Southey wrote of a visit of the whole Wilberforce family to Keswick in 1818 as "a pell-mell, topsy-turvey and chaotic confusion." "His wife (Barbara) sits in the midst of it like Patience on a monument," Southey concludes, "and he frisks about as if every vein in his body were filled with quick-silver."

In 1808 Wilberforce moved from Clapham to Gore House, Kensington. The perpetual oscillation between Clapham and Palace Yard, which he had kept on as a "parliamentary perch," was getting too much for him. His new house, with its ample gardens, stood where the Albert Hall now stands, his guests getting down from their carriages roughly on the site of the Hall's present main entrance. He liked the country air and found he could get through reciting to himself the 119th Psalm in the mile-long walk to Hyde Park Corner. Meanwhile Henry Thornton bought Palace Yard so as to retain a *pied-à-terre* convenient to Parliament. "Mr. Wilberforce, I hope, has forgotten that Palace Yard is no longer his," he wrote wryly to Hannah More, "for he dines here naturally at any hour except ours. . . ."

In order to counteract the ease with which all manner of people would plague him now that he was nearer town, Wilberforce bought a secret little house next door to Gore House, which he nicknamed "The Nuisance." This subterfuge was of course fruitless, for, as Thornton wrote, "He is a man who, were he in Norway or Siberia would find himself infested by company, since he would even produce a population, for the sake of his society, in the regions of the earth where it is least. His heart also is so large that he will never be able to refrain from inviting people to his house."

So it was in Kensington Gore. Breakfast invitations were scattered with even greater profusion, and after breakfast his waiting room became crowded with every kind of petitioner. One of Wilberforce's helpers would move around to discover who was asking for what. Then Wilberforce would appear, bobbing from group to group, greeting, listening and sympathizing. His quicksilver face would register compassion or indignation, or keen appreciation. "Factories did not spring up more rapidly in Leeds or Manchester than schemes of benevolence beneath this roof," reported James Stephen the younger. The house became a kind of national centre for benevolence and moral reform, and he was at this time president, vice-president or committee man of sixty-nine societies. Henry Thornton justly said that he dissipated his usefulness by not sufficiently selecting his beneficiaries.

An important reason for Wilberforce's move to Kensington was his desire to see more of his four sons and two daughters, and this was certainly the main motive for resigning his Yorkshire seat in 1812. He did not want to leave Yorkshire, where he could have sat for the rest of his life, but the heavy correspondence, visits to the North and close attention to constituents were great consumers of precious time, and his health was not improving. The decisive moment may have come when he picked up one of his young sons, who cried. The nurse struck him to the heart by saying, "He is always afraid of strangers." After many agonies, he accepted one of the two seats of the tiny pocket borough of Bramber in Sussex, which Barbara's cousin, Lord Calthorpe, offered him.

Men of Wilberforce's day and class seldom saw much of their children, but Wilberforce had always felt that "the spiritual interests of my children is my first object." Indeed he loved playing with them. "I am irresistibly summoned to a game of marbles," he terminated an early letter. Now at Kensington it was more often blind man's buff or cricket, though his eyesight suited him better for the former than the latter, and a fast ball from his eldest son, William, crippled him for days. He was delighted to have them round him. A friend was with him at Gore House one day when, with rising frustration, he was searching for a lost despatch. Just then the clamour from the nursery above reached a crescendo. The friend thought that now, at last, Wilberforce would give way to irritation. Instead he paused and with a delighted smile remarked, "Only think what a relief, amidst other hurries, to hear their voices and know they are well."

It was at Kensington that his sons grew through boyhood to university age. From the first, his eldest, William, was his main anxiety. He was clever enough and like his father charming, but idle, "without energy of character or solid principle of action." He went to Trinity College, Cambridge, but did little work and was soon led into escapades by undergraduates who thought it rather fun to mislead the celebrated Mr. Wilberforce's son. In his second year he bought a second horse at a steep price, just when he knew his father was having to retrench financially, and it soon became clear that he was lying about the matter. The last straw was when Wilberforce heard that he had been very drunk one night, while his friend Blundell's body lay ready for burial in the next set of rooms. John Venn's son, Henry, who was a Fellow of the College, recommended withdrawing him for a time. Wilberforce found it very hard—"alas my poor Wilm. How sad to be compelled to banish my eldest son" but did so, not as a punishment but for fear that he might become a wastrel. William took it well and the affection between father and son grew rather than diminished. In the end William was put to study for the Bar in the care of the secretary of the Bible Society. He promptly fell in love with the secretary's handsome and penniless daughter, and they were married the next year.

Soon after, Wilberforce sold Gore House, as he could no longer afford it. It was bought for £10,000 by "a Chinaman, or I should say the Keeper of a China shop in Bond St.," to use the novelist Maria Edgeworth's description; a Mr. Mortlake who promptly offered the title deeds back to Wilberforce "as a testimony of esteem." Wilberforce did not accept, but lived in several houses until, after his retirement from Parliament in 1825, he bought Highwood Hill, a house with 140 acres near Millhill.

The three younger boys, Robert, Samuel and Henry, proceeded one after the other to Oriel College, Oxford, then recognized as *the* leading academic College, and all took First Class Honours. "Show me a man who can make the same boast!" commented their delighted father. Samuel and Henry were each President of the infant Oxford Union, Gladstone and Manning being the others in Henry's year. All three became clergymen, while Henry was for a time a Fellow of the College. William, failing at the Bar, decided to farm his father's acres, but he proved a poor farmer and incurred considerable losses.

He then became friendly with a certain Captain Close, who persuaded him—and Wilberforce—that a dairy farm and retail milk business in St. John's Wood was the way to recoup losses on the Highwood farm and occupy William. Although now straitened in circumstances (the building of a church at Highwood had proved expensive) Wilberforce allowed William to invest his inheritance in the venture and himself borrowed £6,000 from a cousin. This proved insufficient, and William borrowed secretly from a moneylender as well as openly from the Thornton bank. The venture ended in debts of £50,000, over half a million in today's currency. It was a seemingly crippling blow to an old, ill man. Wilberforce could have let William bear the loss and be a permanent exile on the Continent, but chose to shoulder the debt himself.

When the facts became known, six of his friends asked to be allowed to pay the debt. To his great credit his old antagonist Lord Fitzwilliam tried to approach Wilberforce through an intermediary, offering to pay the whole amount. The intermediary, knowing Wilberforce's mind, declined to pass on this amazingly generous offer. Wilberforce sold Highwood and let all his servants go except a man, a maid and a reader. He also sold his Yorkshire lands to provide annuities for old servants and his charity pensioners. Henceforth he spent his life moving between his sons' country vicarages. "What gives me repose," he noted in his diary two days after the full facts were revealed, "is the thought of their being His appointment . . . I shall miss most my books and my garden, though I own I do feel a little the not being able to ask my friends to dinner or a bed with me under my own roof." "I can scarce understand why my life has been spared so long," he added later, "except it be to show that a man can be as happy without a fortune as with one." "The stroke was not suffered to fall until all my children are educated and nearly all placed out and by the delay Mrs. Wilberforce and I are supplied with a delightful asylum under the roofs of two of our children. What better could we desire?" he added later. William remained self-justifying till the end, denying that any action of his had proved so ruinous to his father. The relationship between them, however, remained cordial and Wilberforce scraped the bottom of the barrel to give William a new start.

Oriel in his sons' day was full of Fellows who were soon to be the heart of the High Church Oxford Movement.* Wilberforce's sons brought them to Highwood to see their father. He was delighted with John Keble's *The Christian Year*, thought Richard Hurrell Froude "a very out of the way, but very intelligent and extraordinary man" and rejoiced that Henry "enjoyed so much of the society of so excellent a man as Mr. Newman." The friendship between Henry and Newman was one of the formative influences of the early Oxford Movement, and in due course Henry and Robert, as well as

---

*A movement starting in 1833 to revive the Church of England; it had nothing to do with the Oxford Group.

William, joined the Catholic Church. Samuel remained in the Church of England and became a "high church" Bishop of Oxford maintaining that he "only ripened the fruit on his father's tree."

All this was to happen after Wilberforce's death, for Keble's Assize Sermon, the start of the Oxford movement, was preached only two weeks before he died, and the first *Tract for Our Times*, the polemical booklets of the movement, appeared two months afterwards. Wilberforce had used to joke that "my three Oxonians are strong friends to High Church and King Doctrines," but he chiefly loved their pastoral earnestness and disciplined lives. He loved to hear them preach. Sermons, he found, made him sleepy. He counteracted this, Charles Shore relates, by climbing on the front pew and leaning on the pulpit, where he watched Samuel through his eye-glass from a few inches away. There he beamed and nodded and gestured, "quite unaware that every eye in the rustic congregation was fixed upon him."

What he would have deplored was the spiritual combativeness of the Tractarians and the ripostes of the narrower Evangelicals of the 1860s. In this spirit he rebuked Samuel for showing antagonism to Dissenters. While remaining a strong Evangelical, his first love was to help people regardless of religious allegiance to an experience of Christ. He was distressed to hear that his old friend William Smith was off to chair a Unitarian meeting, having hoped he had moved further, but when an elderly fellow-lodger in Bath told him he had been reading *A Practical View*, he tried to show him how he could embrace the most important doctrines of true Christianity and still continue a good Roman Catholic. He had earlier feared Catholicism, though he had favoured Catholics' having the vote and the right to sit in Parliament. In 1832 he actually engaged a Catholic tutor for his grandson William. In fact, while never altering his beliefs, he practised a tolerance a hundred years or more ahead of his times.

17

Slaves Favoured Over Countrymen?

A FREQUENT CRITICISM OF Wilberforce during his lifetime was the alleged contrast between his tireless work for the relief of the West Indian negroes and his record at home where, it was said, he did little or nothing for the poor, as well as supporting repressive Government measures. This view was most memorably publicized by that journalist of genius, William Cobbett, and by the essayist, William Hazlitt. Their conclusion was that he was a hypocrite and their words have been parroted down the years. As late as 1971, a serious biographer writes, "Wilberforce actually opposed legislation intended to improve factory conditions in contemporary England."

Cobbett's attack centred upon Wilberforce's work for the "fat, lazy negroes," while "doing nothing" for the white wage slaves of England. Hazlitt added a more acid charge of duplicity and snobbery. "Mr. Wilberforce," he wrote, "has all the air of the most perfect independence, and gains a character for impartiality and candour, when he is only striking a balance between the *éclat* of differing from a Minister on some vantage ground and the risk or odium that may attend it. . . . His patriotism, his philanthropy are not so ill-bred as to quarrel with his loyalty or to banish him from the first circles. He preaches vital Christianity to untutored savages: and tolerates its worst abuses in civilized states."

Much of Hazlitt's case can be dismissed out of hand. Wilberforce's speeches in the debates on the Prince of Wales' income, the Royal Divorce and the Duke of York scandal (where the Duke's mistress was found to be selling army commissions on a gigantic scale) show that he was no flatterer of the great. He was in fact quite free of social ambition. The people he admired most were men like the Baptist missionary William Carey, who was despised by Sydney Smith as a "consecrated cobbler," and one might as easily meet a butcher or a penniless clergyman as a duke or a banker in his house. He never courted favour—or, if at all, only to assist the causes for which he worked.

Cobbett's complaint was first manufactured by the Slave Trade interest in the earliest days of Wilberforce's crusade. He presumably picked it up when he began his journalistic career as a paid propagandist for the West Indian lobby, and retained his odd view of slavery long after he became a genuine tribune of the people. "I believe our own laws for the treatment of slaves are . . . mild," he wrote as late as 1811. "A *few* lashes: no *effusion of blood*: No contusion even; the number of lashes fixed: even the *degree of force* fixed." For him the slaves were "laughing from morning till night" and their masters "men as gentle as generous and as good as ever breathed." Such words from the man who accused Wilberforce of being "totally ignorant of the subject of slavery" or else "the most consummate hypocrite" illustrate the "extravagance of theory, recklessness of statement and violence of diction" which Trevelyan notes as characteristic of Cobbett's writing.

As an experienced Parliamentary reporter, Cobbett must have known that his statement that Wilberforce had "never done one single act in favour of the labourers of this country" was not true. It was, for example, Wilberforce's colleague

Gisborne, who, in 1794, first focused attention on the fearful conditions endured by children working in factories, declaring that the case "cried loudly for the interference of the Legislature." It was the Society for Bettering the Condition of the Poor,* usually called the Bettering Society and founded in Wilberforce's house, that first called for definite legislation to limit the hours worked by children in the cotton mills, to regulate the age and conditions of apprenticeship and to provide for regular inspection. In 1802 one of its Vice-Presidents, Sir Robert Peel,[†] with strong backing from Wilberforce, carried through a Bill ending forced apprenticeship and forbidding night work for children in the Lancashire cotton mills. It was pitifully small advance in a battle which was only to be won by Wilberforce's successor, Lord Shaftesbury. It was however, scarcely the work of people indifferent to the state of the labouring poor.[‡]

Perhaps Wilberforce and his friends should have done more for British labourers than they did, but one cannot help feeling that there is some justice in Howse's comment that "to reproach a man who spent a life-time of unwearied toil in exterminating one iniquity—the greatest of the day—for not exterminating another is like reproaching Columbus for not

---

*The aim of the Bettering Society was the scientific investigation of the problems of proverty and the spreading information about methods of relief and improvements in conditions. "In pauperism as in slavery, the degradation of character deprives the individual of half his value," its founder, the Evangelical Thomas Bernard said. It stimulated many local societies, and the Royal Institution originated in one of its meetings.

[†]The father of the Victorian Prime Minister. He was at first a bad employer, but later became aware of his employees' wretched state. He not only changed his ways, but faced the humiliation of having his former methods exposed in Parliament when he brought in this Bill.

[‡]One wishes that Cobbett and Wilberforce had met. Wilberforce was a good listener and seldom thought ill of any sincere person whom he met. Cobbett could have taught him much about the developing conditions in industrial England. On the other hand, few people who talked with Wilberforce continued to call him a hypocrite. Thus Sydney Smith, for long one of his most vocal critics, met him in 1827 and wrote to Lady Holland: "Little Wilberforce is here, and we are great friends. He looks like a little spirit running about without a body, or in a kind of undress with only half a body."

also discovering Australia."* Wilberforce's frail frame—and even his moral influence—were already strained to the limit in conducting his major crusades.

Bready points out another connection between Wilberforce's fight and that for factory reform. A great deal of education and preparation was required before a Parliament, tolerant to the Slave Trade and devoted to the rigid *laissez-faire* economics of the day, would contemplate the reformation of the factories. "It must be remembered," he writes, "that both the Commercial Revolution, with its insatiable monetary cupidity, and all the most revolting exploitations of the Industrial Revolution, had already come into being under the influence of the slave trade and under the impact of colonial slavery. Following the Assiento concessions, every economic perversion which later was to manifest itself on the titanic scale of the factory system, was present in the economic and industrial fabric of English society. The slave trade and slavery had contaminated every branch of commercial and financial organisation. The South Sea Bubble itself was but symptomatic of the pervasive and almost universal moral collapse. . . . The first imperative of social emancipation was the renewal of spiritual life; the second was the suppression of the slave trade which, by its manifold repercussions, defiled all trade. Without these preceding achievements, Shaftesbury's intrepid lifework (the reform in the factories) would have been impossible."† It was to these "preceding achievements" which Wilberforce addressed himself.

These facts do not however dispose of the other half of

---

*E. M. Forster, who tended to agree that there was something in Cobbett's criticism, added: "I do not share the moral indignation that sometimes accompanies it. The really bad people, it seems to me, are those who do no good anywhere, and help no one either at home or abroad. There are plenty of them about, and when they are clever as well as selfish they manage to slip through their lives unnoticed, and to escape the censure of historians."

†William Cobbett himself recognized this connection in 1832, when he wrote in the Emancipators' hour of victory, "These slaves are in general the property of the English borough mongers . . . and the fruit of the labour of these slaves has long been converted into the means of making us slaves at home."

the radicals' complaint: that Wilberforce supported unnecessary Government repression. For he did, both in 1794 and in
1816, support the suspension of *Habeas Corpus*, as well as
Pitt's "Gagging Acts" and the Combinations Act which outlawed Trades Unions. Societies he founded and actively
supported also prosecuted (sometimes, to our eyes, callously)
individuals who published books like Paine's *Age of Reason*.

To understand the way Wilberforce viewed these matters,
one needs to realize his absolute devotion to two things: to the
Constitution as it had evolved since the "Glorious Revolution"
of 1688 and to the Christian faith as he understood it. The
"happy Constitution," as Wilberforce called it, had brought a
freedom to the individual Englishman which astonished foreign visitors. "England," wrote Montesquieu after his visit in
1729, "is the freest country in the world. I make no exception
of any republic. I call it free because the sovereign, whose
person is controlled and limited, is unable to inflict any
imaginable harm on anyone." Wilberforce believed in the
principles and social order which had made these liberties
possible, and moreover, as we have seen, thought this life but
a brief prelude to the next and a period in which Christianity
met the needs of every class. Meanwhile he saw in the Terror
across the Channel the inevitable result of trying to achieve
freedom by bloody revolution.

The shock of the French Revolution had indeed been
almost universal among the ruling classes—all the more so
because France had for a century been the model of European
civilization. The fear that such chaos might also engulf England
was all too real. Thus Gibbon wrote to Lord Sheffield:

> Do not suffer yourselves to be deluded into a false security;
> remember the proud fabric of the French monarchy. Not four
> years ago it stood founded, as it might seem, on the rock of
> time, force and opinion, supported by the triple Aristocracy
> of the Church, the Nobility and the Parliaments. They are
> crumbled into dust; they are vanished from the earth. If this
> tremendous warning has no effect on the men of property in

England; if it does not open every eye and raise every arm,
you will deserve your fate.

In addition, Wilberforce believed that the central test of a
country's spiritual health, and hence its happiness, was
whether it really believed in and practised true Christianity.
Thus in 1792 he wrote: "I will frankly own that I entertain
rather gloomy apprehensions concerning the state of the
country. Not that I fear a speedy commotion—of this I own I
see no danger . . . But I do see a gathering storm and I cannot
help fearing that a country which, like this, has so long been
blessed beyond all example with every spiritual and temporal
good, will incur those judgements of an incensed God which in
the Prophets are often denounced against those who forget
the Author of all their mercies." Without vital religion a country
would ultimately be doomed.

To this fear—whether reasonable or not—of atheist
authoritarianism can be traced most of Wilberforce's support
for repressive measures. In 1794 he backed Pitt's suspension
of *Habeas Corpus* at a time when the nation was, as he
believed, threatened both by France's revolutionary armies
and by an atheist ideology which seemed to be taking root at
many levels in Britain. His was no *carte blanche* support, for it
was given at almost the same time as he was bitterly offending
Pitt by advocating a peace initiative. By October 1795, after
Pitt had come round to his way of thinking but was frustrated
by French intransigence, Wilberforce supported him again in
his so-called "Gagging Bills" as unfortunate wartime necessi-
ties.

These two Bills—one against treasonable and seditious
practices, the other to prevent seditious meetings, but not
censoring the Press, touching the Parliamentary Opposition or
affecting the right to petition—were passed by an overwhelming majority as temporary wartime measures. Certainly the
prospect seemed grim enough. Military failures and a bad
harvest had brought war-weariness and hunger, and the
resultant discontent looked to most MPs like an attempt to start

a revolution in wartime. Many feared it could lead to a Reign of Terror and the introduction of a Committee of Public Safety on the French model, even—such were some of his State-ments—headed by Fox. The mob was out, reminiscent of the Gordon Riots of 1780, and when a stone shattered the window of the state Coach as the King was on his way to open Parliament, he entered the House saying, "I have been shot at." It was in this atmosphere that the Bills were proposed and passed.

Wilberforce supported them because he felt that protests in wartime should be made either in the House of Commons or at assemblies in the counties sanctioned by Lord Lieuten-ants or Sheriffs, requests for which should not be lightly refused. In Yorkshire his old ally, Christopher Wyvill, tried to secure such a meeting of the freeholders to condemn the "Gagging Bill," but the Sheriff refused to allow it. Wilberforce deplored this suppression of a debate, which was quite legal even after the passing of the new Acts, and, when Wyvill persisted in holding a meeting, he decided he must go to York to argue the Government's case. As his own coach was not prepared, he took Pitt's chariot and four, which caused one Cabinet Minister to remark: "If they find out whose carriage you have got, you will run the risk of being murdered." As he thundered north, dictating his speech as he went, he did not know what to expect, but when he arrived at the Guildhall a great cheer went up and hats were thrown in the air. Wilber-force addressed a meeting adjourned to Castle Yard. "I never felt the power of eloquence until that day," wrote Colonel Cockell later. "You breathed energy and vigour into the desponding souls of timid loyalists, and sent us home with joy and delight." Wilberforce himself was back in Parliament two winter days later and presented the overwhelming Yorkshire address of confidence.

The Combination Act of 1799 was actually suggested by Wilberforce, though he took no part in its framing or in the debate about it. In common with most of his contemporaries—and he was very much a man of his times, even though so far ahead in many matters—he thought of the combination of workers in the middle of the French wars as a step towards revolution. Magnanimity from the rich and resignation from the poor was very much the order of the day, and he regarded himself as on the workers' side in guarding them from "agitators" and in awakening the conscience of the ruling classes. The Act was, in the event, little used and was repealed twenty-five years later. Meanwhile, the early Trades Unions were able, to some extent, to shelter behind the Friendly Societies Act introduced by Wilberforce and a colleague.

His part in the suppression of Tom Paine's *The Age of Reason*, which outrages the modern mind, sprang from the fact that he saw it as an attempt to destroy both the constitution and the Christian religion. Of the two, the latter was to him the more important. Thus, later, he showed considerable interest in Robert Owen's socialist theories for the well-being of the worker in his New Lanark factory, but when Owen came out unmistakably against Christianity, Wilberforce sided with Owen's Quaker partner, William Allen, and voted against referring Owen's theories to a Commons Committee. Pollock comments: "Any other course would have been inconsistent. Owen acknowledged this, but the early twentieth-century Fabian writers shook their heads sadly that Wilberforce should oppose a reformer merely because he excluded religion. These Fabians who wrote at the end of an age of social progress which was based, thanks partly to Wilberforce, on Christian ethical standards and principles, failed to foresee what happens when a nation rejects religion. A century or so later men knew about the crushing of freedom of thought in atheist Soviet Russia." Wilberforce hated and saw the consequences which would flow from State atheism. He did not hate atheists; but his hatred of the principle did sometimes override his otherwise universal humanity towards individuals.

After the war, when Liverpool and Sidmouth were in power, Wilberforce again lent himself to the suspension of *Habeas Corpus* and other repressive legislation. This was during the agitations caused by the passing of the Corn Laws.

The price of corn had fallen heavily and seemed to portend the collapse of British agriculture, still by far the nation's largest industry and the one overwhelmingly represented in Parliament. Wilberforce, after much heart-searching, voted for the Corn Laws, which prevented the importing of corn until its price rose beyond 80 shillings a quarter, although he wished the limit to be placed slightly lower. The price of bread rose, which helped British agriculture but threw working people in the cities into terrible distress.

On November 15th, 1816, an enormous crowd met in Spa Fields and signed a petition to the Prince Regent. Hunt, the meeting's radical spokesman, twice tried to deliver the petition and was twice turned away. On December 2nd, when the meeting was reconvened, a group of more serious revolutionaries broke away and marched into the city, killing a gunsmith *en route*. It was a small affair as riots go, but the presence of the tricolour flag and the cap of liberty brought memories of the Terror, and when, at the opening of Parliament in January 1817, the Prince Regent's coach was stoned, as George III's had been in 1795, the Cabinet swiftly tightened the law. A secret committee of which Wilberforce was a member received reports of a plot to carry out a revolution by force of arms, and once more recommended the temporary suspension of *Habeas Corpus* and severe restrictions on public meetings. Six months later it became clear that much of the evidence laid before the Committee had been fraudulent, and came from an *agent provocateur. Habeas Corpus* was restored.

The harvest of 1817 was good and the unrest seemed to abate, but it was a false dawn. The following year brought a new recession, which caused even greater distress. The Government replied with greater repression, which led to the Massacre of Peterloo, when eleven were killed and several hundred wounded by a troop of hussars in an unjustifiably violent response to a demonstration for reform. Again the Government stiffened the law.

Wilberforce supported the Government. The radicals

resented his support of such legislation far more than that of
men like Liverpool and Sidmouth from whom, they felt,
nothing better could be expected. This, together with the way
he had backed Pitt earlier and certain cases in which he
supported the prosecution of authors and publishers for
blasphemy, was what led to the bitter contrasting of his
support for liberty abroad and the use of his moral authority to
oppose it at home.

The plain fact is that Wilberforce did not understand the
intolerable strains which the Industrial Revolution and the rise
in food prices placed upon British workers. He also, because of
long association, placed a naive trust in men like Sidmouth
which he would never have done during the battle over the
Slave Trade. Then, of course, he had the assistance of his
"white negroes" and examined every question personally in
the minutest detail. Now he was unable to investigate personally—Barbara prevented him from travelling—and was more
and more dependent on his correspondents, many of them
conservatively-minded clergy, who were forever telling him of
conspirators who were out to undermine the Constitution and
overthrow religion. His worsening eyesight even closed the
newspapers, with their tiny print, to him, and he found being
read to an increasingly wearying occupation. No doubt, too,
he tended to get more rather than less conservative as he got
older. So he became an easy victim of old associates like
Sidmouth who attributed all unrest to agitators. "The owning
and personal control of one small factory would have taught
him much," writes Oliver Warner. "It is fair to think that he
would have treated his work-people like a family, since he was
never less than generous in his dealing with his fellow-men.
Denied that enlightening experience, he spoke and acted as
one who was too often content to let the affairs of State be
managed by others less scrupulous than himself." He should
have been more suspicious of men like Sidmouth and Liverpool, for they had often obstructed his fight against the Slave
Trade and slavery.

Whenever he saw distress, however, he was swift to try

and lessen it. All the Clapham brotherhood gave until it hurt to help the needy, sacrificing most luxuries to do so in a way which it is hard to imagine any of their Whig critics emulating. Thornton, for example, gave away at least five-sixths of his income each year while he was single and more than a quarter when he had a large family to bring up. Wilberforce gave away a third until marriage—in one year indeed, £3,000 more than his income—and a considerable slice each year after marriage, and usually anonymously. They believed that needs were better met by voluntary giving than by compulsion, though Wilberforce once advocated a Wealth Tax and, whenever he bought a property, used to reduce the rent by thirty or forty per cent or, if times were bad, waived it altogether. His response to poverty was personal* and emotional rather than doctrinal. He did not believe that poverty should be answered by remodelling the social and economic order, but felt an overwhelming personal responsibility both to relieve human suffering and to call the rich and powerful to do the same.

However, by tackling the Slave Trade he and his friends had made the first breach in the *laissez-faire* system of economics. When the evil was large enough, they believed, State intervention was essential, whether it was the Slave Trade, the conditions of the climbing boys who worked for the chimney sweeps, or the exploitation in the cotton mills. This approach was continued after their deaths by younger disciples, like Lord Shaftesbury, so that the Evangelicals could claim to be, as Bradley points out, "the only people who formulated a coherent argument on which to base Government interference." In place of *laissez- faire*, they offered the

---

*Lord Clarendon recalled a typical case. "I was with him once when he was preparing an important motion in the House of Commons. While he was most deeply engaged, a poor man called, I think his name was Simkins, who was in danger of being imprisoned for a small debt. Wilberforce did not like to become his security without inquiry; it was contrary to a rule he had made but nothing could induce him to send the man away. 'His goods,' said he, 'will be seized and the poor fellow will be totally ruined.' I believe at last he paid the debt himself; but remember well the interruption which it gave to his business, which he would not resume till the case was provided for."

philosophy of paternalism, which was, Bradley adds, "a distinctive contribution to the development of the Welfare State in Britain." Wilberforce's success in abolishing the Slave Trade gave a strong impetus to that development. After Abolition, the feeling grew that any abuse could be reformed, if fought against hard enough. Abolition in that sense was, as O. A. Sharrard says, "the parent stem from which all other reforms sprang."

Meanwhile Wilberforce was consistently fighting to better the condition of the poor. He fought for their education, maintaining several schools out of his own pocket. With Arthur Young, he conceived a number of schemes for producing better, cheaper food. In 1800 he wrote to Young of his shock at the "languor which prevails on this important subject" among his colleagues on the Commons Scarcity Committee. To Muncaster, he added: "Our first report is made. Alas! it does not go far enough. I wish that we should gain the hearts of our people by declaring our determination to abridge our luxuries and comforts and superfluities not merely bread. This way of establishing a distinction between rich and poor in times like these is neither prudent nor feeling. They compare our situation to that of a ship at short allowance; but then the officers are at short allowance too, not only the men." In December 1819 he suggested "the employment in public works for large numbers of the working class. The disproportion between demand for the labour and the number of labourers would thus be lessened, by which wages would materially rise."

He also attacked the Game Laws, so dear to most Members, and fought against "our murderous laws" and the "barbarous custom of hanging." On these issues he played a supporting role to reformers like Romilly and Mackintosh. When Romilly committed suicide, he stepped into the gap and presented the Quakers' petition to limit hanging to the most serious crimes, and it was he who was largely responsible for getting Sir James Mackintosh to take Romilly's place in the fight for penal reform. He also co-operated actively with

Bentham and Howard on prison reform, visited Newgate with Elizabeth Fry and bombarded the Home Secretary on her behalf. And even his remorseless Sabbatarianism had a social content—for thus only was it ensured that workers were not forced to work seven days every week.

On the question of Parliamentary Reform, too, Wilberforce was by no means as inactive as his critics alleged. Hazlitt's cry, "What have the *Saints* to do with freedom or reform of any kind?" was singularly ill-informed. Wilberforce had, as we have seen, worked for reform from his earliest days in Parliament. He had initiated several plans and persevered long after Pitt, for instance, wearied in well-doing. Indeed, the Saints voted for reform again and again, though not for so sudden a variety as Cobbett and his friends wished. One of Wilberforce's reasons for opposing the French war in 1785 was that it would delay reform and, even in 1831, when he had long left politics, he expressed himself strongly in favour of Lord John Russell's Bill, partly because a reformed house would be more favourable to the freeing of the slaves.

Furthermore, Wilberforce and his friends established the charitable society as the principal means of doing good in the Victorian era. To them Britain owes the tradition, still strong today, of voluntary service by unpaid workers supported by voluntary gifts from individuals. This, incidentally, gave many women the chance of useful social work for the first time. Lucy Aikin, writing in 1841, attributes the change to the influence of Sarah Trimmer and Hannah More:

> This philanthropic impulse acted at first chiefly within the Evangelical party; but that party became, at length, great enough to give the tone to society at large; and the practice of superintending the poor has become so general, that I know no one circumstance by which the manners, studies and occupations of Englishwomen have been so extensively modified, or so strikingly contradistinguished from those of a former generation.

Philanthropy, noted Lord Shaftesbury in the same year, had become fashionable. Of course there was often an unpleasant sense of patronage involved, a sentiment peculiarly repugnant in this twentieth century. Bradley is undeniably right, however, when he points out that "a society where do-gooding is fashionable is preferable to one where the want and suffering of the poor is ignored, as had at least partly been the case in England until the Evangelicals helped to awaken the consciences of their countrymen."

18

Freeing the Slaves

IN ALL THESE YEARS, of course, Wilberforce's major preoccupation was still the slaves. The 1807 Act had legally abolished the British Slave Trade. To pass such an Act was a magnificent achievement, but to approach the position where its provisions were observed—and adopted worldwide—entailed many years' more work. The situation looked favourable immediately after the triumphant Abolition debate, for America and Denmark had already abolished the Trade, while France, Spain and Holland were prevented from active trading by the war. Portugal was the only nation actually conducting a large legal trade in slaves.

Full of optimism, the men of Clapham felt they could now turn their attention to a constructive task very dear to their hearts: making reparation, where they could, to the continent of Africa. Ever since 1787, when they had founded the settlement in Sierra Leone to absorb the slaves on English soil freed after Chief Justice Mansfield's judgement in the *Somerset* case, they had been working to sustain that infant colony. The first settlement had been a disaster, due largely to

Granville Sharp's impractical direction; but, in spite of numerous setbacks, the settlement had been maintained continuously after the founding of the Sierra Leone Company in 1791, with Thornton and Wilberforce in effective control in London. There was still a series of revolts in the colony, as well as a devastating raid by a French squadron in 1794, but from the time when Zachary Macaulay became Governor, Sierra Leone made steady progress. In 1799, when he finally returned to Britain, Macaulay left a thriving community of 1,200 people, half of them supported by their own farms. The capital, Freetown, contained 300 houses, with public buildings and three wharves to facilitate foreign trade. Sierra Leone was no longer an experiment, but an accomplished fact.

The whole venture had been one of great importance to the Abolitionists. It had shown that relations between England and West Africa could rest on something more wholesome than the Slave Trade. It demonstrated that slaves could hold down positions of responsibility and that Africa had products other than human flesh which the world needed.

On the day that legal trading ended under the 1807 Act, Sierra Leone was turned over by the Company to the British Crown. At the same time its founders established the African Institute to continue and widen the work begun there. Its aim was "to concert means for improving the opportunity, presented by the Abolition of the Slave Trade, for promoting innocent commerce and civilisation in Africa." The Duke of Gloucester became its President, Wilberforce Vice-President, with Babington, Clarkson, Grant, Macaulay, Sharp, Smith and Stephen as Directors, and Thornton as Treasurer. "The chief labour, as in most cases," stated the *Christian Observer*, "fell on Mr. Macaulay."

Within months of the founding of the Institute, it became clear that the illegal smuggling of slaves was continuing on such a large scale that the Abolitionists' main effort would have to be diverted to making the Abolition Act work and to getting it adopted by foreign countries. The British Government, under their pressure, took successive steps to forward these

ends. It sent a small squadron of warships to the slave coasts
to intercept illegal traders and in 1809 issued an Order-in-
Council authorizing the searching of Portuguese ships on the
high seas. In 1810 a treaty was signed with Portugal whereby,
in return for a handsome capital sum, that country forbade her
subjects to ply the Slave Trade in parts of Africa not belonging
to Portugal. Also in 1810, Parliament made slave-trading by
British subjects a felony punishable by transportation for 14
years. Nonetheless, the results were still disappointing: the
illegal trade continued.

Again it was James Stephen who hit upon the method
which was finally to defeat the illegal trade. He proposed the
establishment in the West Indies of an official register of all
slaves, and in January 1812 the Prime Minister, Perceval,
issued an Order-in-Council authorizing a pilot scheme in
Trinidad. Wilberforce and his friends set to work to draft a Bill
making this order applicable in all the islands, but the defeat of
Napoleon in 1814 led them to shelve this Registry Bill in the
hope that their object might be universally achieved through a
general peace treaty.

Wilberforce at once wrote to Tsar Alexander and also to
Talleyrand and Lafayette soliciting their support. At the same
time he obtained a Commons motion instructing the Cabinet
to seek backing for the immediate abolition of the Trade from
all European sovereigns. At the Peace negotiations, however,
Lord Castlereagh found the French obdurate and soon gave
up the battle. He returned with his peace treaty to a jubilant
House but, immediately the applause died down, Wilberforce
rose and described the agreement as "the death warrant of a
multitude of innocent victims."

The men of Clapham turned once more to the country,
and in thirty-four days 800 petitions with almost a million
signatures—a tenth of the entire population—reached Westminster. Seeing "the whole country is bent on it," Castlereagh
went to the Congress of Vienna with a new determination,
flanked this time by the Duke of Wellington who from simple
feelings of justice was in favour of Abolition. Once more,

however, the French Royalists were obdurate, not least because the demand came from England. A reluctant promise to stop slave trading north of the Niger was the only result.

Then what seemed like a miracle took place. Napoleon, returning from Elba, proclaimed the immediate and total Abolition of the Trade, in a bid to win Britain's favour. In that he failed, but when the Congress of Vienna reassembled after Waterloo, Louis XVIII, restored by British arms, had no choice but to confirm Napoleon's gesture. A declaration by the eight powers that they would abolish the Trade as swiftly as possible was annexed to the final Treaty signed on June 9th, 1815. In a hundred years, since the Assiento Clause had been obtained in the Treaty of Utrecht in 1714, British diplomacy had made one of the boldest U-turns in history. However, the smuggling of slaves continued, and even the paying of £400,000 compensation to Spain (as earlier with Portugal) did not solve the problem. Only the British Navy, a sixth of which was deployed for the purpose, seriously attempted to enforce the Congress' decision.

On February 15th, meanwhile, Wilberforce's "Cabinet Council" had met and decided to press ahead with the Registry Bill. The Government procrastinated, and the fiery Stephen was so disgusted that he resigned from the House in protest. Wilberforce and the others continued, but Castlereagh induced them to wait for a year while attempts were made to get the colonial legislatures to adopt registration measures of their own accord. Simultaneously, the West Indian interests conducted a vast campaign against the measure, even levying a voluntary tax on every hogshead of sugar to finance the fight against it. So the Registry Bill never did get off the ground.

As a sop to Britain the colonial legislatures did in fact pass registry acts of their own, while not of course enforcing them. Finally the British Government, spurred on by the men of Clapham, lost patience, and the Secretary of the Colonies introduced a measure establishing a register of colonial slaves, to be maintained in Britain. The colonies, having already paid lip service to the idea, could not object, and so the whole aim of the Registry Act was adroitly achieved. Wilberforce wrote joyfully to Macaulay, "No one has more right than you to be congratulated for no one else has done or suffered so much in and for this great cause."

Both the extent of evasion and the horrors revealed during the fight for registration now determined the Abolitionists to proceed towards full Emancipation. Individual cases had come to light which did more to rouse public opinion than statistics, however horrifying. Thus in one case a planter was found to have sentenced two slave boys to a hundred lashes for allegedly receiving a stolen pair of stockings and their sister to thirty for shedding tears when she saw her brothers beaten. The Attorney-General proceeded against the planter, but a local jury acquitted him. In another case, a runaway slave was caught, flogged and set to work, chained to another slave. He complained of pain and hunger, but was flogged back onto his feet in the presence of the estate manager, a Revd. Mr. Rawlins. During the course of the day the slave died, still chained to his fellow. A coroner's jury sent down the absurd verdict, "Died by the visitation of God," presumably on the theory that Mr. Rawlins was God's representative. When the news reached England, the Attorney-General insisted that Rawlins be tried. He was duly found guilty of manslaughter, and sent to prison for three months with a fine of £200. The British Government remained unappeased, and the Colonial Secretary wrote bluntly to the Governor that "Mr. Rawlins could not have been guilty of manslaughter: it must either have been murder or an acquittal."

Such cases inflamed British public opinion. The West Indian interest, on the other hand, mounted an unprecedented campaign of character assassination, mainly aimed at Wilberforce. They hoped to wear him down, even as they had hounded Ramsay to his death years before, but Wilberforce was of tougher mettle and his reputation in the country was such that he was not now so easily defamed. The climax of this campaign came in an Open Letter by William Cobbett. Wilberforce, having formed the new Anti-Slavery Society, had in 1823 written his *Appeal to the Religion, Justice and Humanity of the Inhabitants of the British Empire on Behalf of the Negro Slaves in the West Indies*, which, together with Stephen's *Slavery Delineated*, became the textbook of the Emancipators. Cobbett, much of whose letter was concerned with the grievous state of the British cotton workers, called Wilberforce's *Appeal* "a great deal of canting trash: a great deal of lying: a great deal of cool impudent falsehood for which the Quakers are famed . . . There is no man who knows anything at all of the real situation of the Blacks who will not declare you totally ignorant of the subject on which you are writing, or to be a most consummate hypocrite." He contrasted the wretched physical condition of the Lancashire millhands with what he believed to be that of the Blacks: "You seem to have great affection for the fat and lazy and laughing and singing negroes . . .", whereas Cobbett cared for the downtrodden white "wage slaves." "Never," he added, "have you done one single act in favour of the labourers of this country." No wonder John Gladstone, the future Prime Minister's father who owned slaves but treated them well, thought Cobbett a powerful propagandist for the planters.

Wilberforce was not deterred. "I get to be less touchy as to my character," he wrote to Stephen. To abolish property rights was, he knew, far more serious than prohibiting the import of slaves, and the slaves themselves delayed reform by a series of revolts which were rigorously suppressed and used as ammunition against the Emancipators. The ranks of the Clapham old guard had meanwhile been thinned. Henry Thornton, Granville Sharp and John Venn had died, and Wilberforce himself, now over sixty, was in constant ill-health. In May 1821 he asked Thomas Fowell Buxton, an Evangelical like himself and a brother-in-law of Elizabeth Fry, to take his place at the head of the campaign. Nevertheless, on March 19th, 1823, he opened the struggle by presenting on behalf of the Quakers a petition praying Parliament to take measures to redeem the slaves. Canning, then Leader of the House, out-generalled him, and no debate resulted. "Fatigue rather stupified me and I forgot my main points," Wilberforce admitted, even wondering if God, whom he had invoked beforehand, had forsaken him.

In the great debate which followed in May, when Buxton, with Wilberforce at his side, moved that slavery was "repugnant" to the principles of the British constitution and of the Christian religion, Canning once more out-generalled them with small concessions. Then the stupidity of the Colonial governments came to the Abolitionists' aid. One of the British Government's concessions was that slaves must no longer be whipped to make them work. In relaying this instruction to the slaves, the West Indian authorities failed to make it clear that the ending of this symbol of slavery did not mean immediate emancipation. As a result a revolt broke out in Demarara and a Methodist minister named Smith was thrown into prison on a charge of fomenting the insurrection. He was not executed, but the prison conditions were made so severe that he died. Smith immediately became the Anti-Slavery martyr. Brougham brought the case to Parliament in a speech of great power, and Wilberforce, who had just suffered a severe illness, dragged himself to the Commons for what was to be his last speech there. He was disappointed with his performance, but relieved to have "delivered my soul."

Again the well-oiled machine of agitation went into motion. Macaulay composed from official colonial records a devastating picture of Negro Slavery and, on Midsummer Day 1824, experienced "perhaps the happiest day of my life," when his son Thomas, the future Lord Macaulay, made his first anti-slavery speech at the first anniversary meeting of the Anti-Slavery Society. The applause was thunderous as Stephen and Wilberforce held the future historian's hands aloft, while the Duke of Gloucester, in the chair, found it hard to keep back his tears. Wilberforce ended his speech with a reference to the veterans. "We have been engaged in many a long and arduous contest, and we have also had to contend with calumny and falsehood," he said. "But we are more than repaid, by the success that has already attended our efforts, and by the anticipations which we may derive from what we have witnessed this very day, when, if our sun is setting, we see that other luminaries are arising to shine with far greater lustre and more efficient strength."

Next day Wilberforce had an attack of his old bowel trouble. Barbara and he were due to stay with Admiral Gambier, but, by the time he reached Gambier's house at Iver in Buckinghamshire, he had to be helped to bed. Barbara renewed her pressure for him to resign from the House and finally, in February 1825, he capitulated. He arranged to go through the traditional procedure for resigning his seat in the House of Commons, and was promptly offered elevation to the House of Lords as a peer. This he refused as "carving too much for myself." He believed that, through the recruitment of younger Members, his friends were, in spite of the deaths of so many, stronger in the House than at any time since the days when Pitt and Fox spoke with him—and far stronger in the country. "I rejoice to think that I am not wanted," he wrote to Buxton. "The Carthaginians put upon Hannibal's tomb, 'We vehemently desired him in the day of battle,' which exactly describes my feelings," Buxton replied.

Buxton soldiered on with annual motions in the years after Wilberforce's retirement, but little came of them. "The progress of the colonies," said Brougham in 1828, "is so slow as to be imperceptible to all eyes save their own," but anti-slavery opinion was still gaining ground in the country and a new breed of young militant, typified by Stephen's younger son, George, was coming to the fore. They helped to gather a crowd of 2,000 for the 1830 Anti-Slavery meeting, where Clarkson proposed that Wilberforce take the chair. Wilberforce, frail, bent and his voice much weakened, replied with a tribute to his "old friend and fellow-labourer." Buxton made an admirable if prudent speech, pledging to leave "no proper and practical means unattempted for effecting, at the earliest period, the entire abolition of slavery throughout the British dominions." A Mr. Pownell jumped up in a side gallery, and, in defiance of shouts of "Order!" moved the amendment, "That from and after the 1st of January 1830, every slave born in the King's dominions shall be free." It set the meeting on fire. "Cheers innumerable thundered from every bench, hats and handkerchiefs were waved in every hand," records George.

> Buxton deprecated, Brougham interposed, Wilberforce waved his hand for silence, but all was pantomime and dumb show. I did my best in a little knot of some half-dozen men to resist all attempts at suppression. We would allow no silence and no appeals. At the first subsidence of the tempest we began again, reserving our lungs till others were tired. We soon became the bugle-men of the mighty host, nor did we rest, or allow others to rest, till Wilberforce rose to put the amendment, which was carried with a burst of exulting triumph that would have made the Falls of Niagara inaudible at equal distance.

A General Election took place in 1830. Yorkshire was now entitled to four county Members and returned four Abolitionists, including Brougham. "The election turned very much on slavery," he wrote to Wilberforce. "Your name was on every mouth and your health the most enthusiastically received."

Meanwhile the young Abolitionists were setting a new pace. They split themselves off into the Agency Committee, and adopted entirely new tactics, which were in effect a criticism of their elders. For example, before the 1832 election, they advertised in the press lists of parliamentary candidates marked "Anti"—young William Gladstone, later to be four times Liberal Prime Minister, was one of these—"Doubtful" and "Recommended." Only the generosity of such elders as Stephen, Wilberforce and Macaulay kept the movement united. One old campaigner said to young George Stephen, "I have served a long apprenticeship in agitation, my young

friend, but you are my master." The first reformed parliament*
would in any case have returned a large number of Abolitionists, but the Agency's tactics increased the proportion.

After the election the petitions began to flow in again.
Wilberforce was persuaded to propose a petition against
slavery at Maidstone on April 12th, 1833. "I had never
thought to appear in public again," he began, "but it shall
never be said that William Wilberforce is silent while the slaves
require his help." As he spoke, standing there tiny and twisted
and almost lost in his cloak, something of his old spirit seemed
suddenly to take possession of him, and he was, as his sons
wrote, "restored again to some of that clarion character which
had aroused slumbering parliaments." Then, as he concluded,
a beam of sunshine suddenly lit the hall, just as another beam
had illumined the House of Commons forty-two years before
as Pitt finished his greatest speech on Abolition. Catching the
gleam and weaving it into his speech, as Pitt had done, he
cried out that this "light from heaven" was the "earnest of
success."

The day of victory was coming. Stephen died in 1832 and
did not see it. Clarkson and Macaulay lived on, though
Macaulay was too ill on the actual day of triumph to know of
it. But Wilberforce, on his death bed, heard the news,
rejoicing. Parliament had decreed that all slaves in the Empire
were to be freed in one year's time though they must then
serve seven years' apprenticeship with their former masters.
Their masters were given £20 million compensation. "Thank
God," said Wilberforce, "that I should have lived to witness a
day when England is willing to give twenty millions sterling for
the Abolition of Slavery."

"It is a singular fact," said Buxton afterwards, "that on the
very night on which we were successfully engaged in the
House of Commons, in passing the clause of the Act of
Emancipation—one of the most important clauses ever en-

*The great Reform Bill was passed in 1832.

acted . . . the spirit of our friend left the world. The day which was the termination of his labours was the termination of his life."

Wilberforce had been ailing for months. When his much-loved daughter, Lizzie, had died in childbirth in 1832, he said: "I have often heard that sailors on a voyage will drink to 'friends astern' until they are half way over, then to 'friends ahead.' With me it has become 'friends ahead' this long time."

His last stay in a son's home was in Robert's vicarage at East Farleigh, only a mile from Barham Court, where Lady Middleton had pleaded with him fifty years before to take on the cause of Abolition. But his doctor advised him first to move to Bath and then, in July 1833, to London to be under the care of Dr. Chambers. There he shocked friends by the change of his appearance but was as ever in cheerful mood. "I see much in the state of the world and of the church which I deplore, yet I am not among the croakers," he told John Jay, the dissenting preacher. "I think real religion is spreading." His optimism was justified, and his life had been a major encouragement for it. "Wilberforce would disclaim the credit," writes Pollock, "but the essentials of his beliefs and of his conscience formed the foundation of the British character for the next two generations at least. He was proof that a man may change his times, though he cannot do it alone."

With Henry, he had now settled into a cousin's house at 44 Cadogan Place. The Second Reading of the Abolition of Slavery Debate was still in progress and each morning Wilberforce took the air for ten minutes in a bath-chair before family prayers and breakfast at 10. Two young men came to see him in those last July days. One was Gladstone, whom Henry brought to breakfast on the 26th. The event had a deeper significance because Gladstone's slave-owning father was the leader of the West Indian interest in London. His own first major speech in the House, a few weeks earlier, had been in defence of his father's estate manager, whom Lord Howick had called a "murderer of slaves," and against the too-sudden freeing of the slaves. Gladstone was deeply touched by the encounter. "He is cheerful and serene, a beautiful picture of old age in sight of immortality," he noted in his diary. "Heard him pray with his family. Blessing and honour are upon his head."

Ten days after his visit to Cadogan Place, Gladstone attended Wilberforce's funeral in Westminster Abbey. "It brought me solemn thoughts, particularly about the slaves. This is a burdensome question," he noted. Years later he was to record, "I can see plainly enough the sad defects, the real illiberalism of my opinions on that subject." So, in death as in life, Wilberforce moulded Britain's leaders.

The other visitor was Thomas Macaulay, who had of course known Wilberforce all his life. He saw him last on the 27th, two days before he died. Wilberforce had just heard of the victory over Emancipation. "He exulted in the success . . . as much as the youngest and most ardent partisan," Macaulay wrote. "He was a very good friend to me and I loved him much." To his sister he added, "Wilberforce kept his faculties, and (except when he was actually in fits), his spirits, to the very last. He was cheerful and full of anecdotes only last Saturday. He owned that he enjoyed life much and that he had a great desire to live longer. Strange in a man who had, I should have said, so little to attach him to this world, and so firm a belief in another: in a man with an impaired fortune, a weak spine, and a worn-out stomach! . . . I was truly fond of him."

That day, Saturday, Wilberforce suddenly became weaker and on Sunday sank rapidly. Late that night, Henry and Barbara heard him whisper: "I am in a very distressed state." "Yes," said Henry, "but you have your feet on the Rock." "I do not venture to speak so positively," Wilberforce murmured humbly, "but I hope I have." At 3 a.m. he died.

19

Statesman Lost—or Found?

AT THEIR FIRST TALK after Wilberforce's conversion, Pitt was afraid that Britain had lost a statesman. But was it a case of a statesman lost or a statesman found?

Wilberforce himself must sometimes have wondered. "Often on my visits to Holwood [Pitt's country house] when I heard one or another speak of this man's place or that man's peerage, I felt a rising inclination to pursue the same objects," he recalled in old age, "but a Sunday in solitude never failed to restore me to myself." If one remembers Trevelyan's estimate—that "with all his talents he would probably have been Pitt's successor as Prime Minister if he had preferred party to mankind"—one can imagine that the temptation was keen. But his commitment was clear. As Isaac Milner reminded him in 1793, "If you carry this [Abolition] in your whole life, that life will be far better spent than in being Prime Minister for many years."

Milner was right—in immediate terms as well as in the eye of history. Whether Wilberforce would have made a good Prime Minister we do not know: his cousin, Bob Carrington, considered his "inaccurate method of doing business" rendered him unfit for any office. But we do know that the passing of the Abolition Act brought him a unique prestige and influence. From being, in Churchill's phrase, "Pitt's conscience," he became a kind of national conscience. He was secure for life, if he so desired, in his Yorkshire constituency, in spite of the limitless money and interest of those who had previously worked to displace him. In Parliament, Pitt's successors were as anxious for his support as Pitt had been. In 1807, for example, when the Whigs hoped to bring down the new Portland Government, Lord Howick was instructed that the motion must be worded and the mover so express himself as to "ensure the support of Wilberforce, Bankes, etc., upon whose opinion much depends." Similar action was taken again and again by Ministers in the years which followed.

Pollock has headed his account of Wilberforce's last eighteen years in Parliament with the words "Arbiter of England." Friend and foe certainly turned to him in times of crisis as to no one else. When in 1809 Castlereagh and Canning fought a duel, and Lord Camden was blamed for having supplied the facts which caused the encounter, Camden brought the evidence to Wilberforce for judgement. He acquitted Camden, but added: "The most unpleasant reflections arising out of the affair are such as impute, to all of you, that you were attending only to each others' personal feelings and not to the public interest." Later, in 1812, he strove to persuade Canning to swallow his dislike of Castlereagh and join the same Ministry. "How much should a man be willing to give up for the good of his country?" he asked Canning, but in vain. If Canning had listened and accepted the Foreign Office, which was offered to him, he would have saved himself a great deal of heartache and would have represented Britain at the Congress of Vienna.

Later, when Queen Caroline came to England to claim her "rights," and when she and her husband George IV became locked in legal warfare, someone as sceptical as the future Lord Melbourne implored Wilberforce to mediate. "If there is anything to be done," he said, "your presence and influence will do it."

Southey wrote that Wilberforce's was the greatest name in the land. "When Mr. Wilberforce passes through the crowd," an Italian diplomat remarked of an opening of Parliament, "everyone contemplates this little old man, worn with age and head sunk in his shoulders, as a sacred relic—as the Washington of humanity." After Waterloo, in particular, many of the crowned heads of Europe treated him as such. Tsar Alexander saw him several times and as late as 1822 Wilberforce's standing with him was such that he could challenge him both privately and publicly to make good his promises on the Slave Trade. His private letter to the Tsar on that occasion was, he reported, "though civil in terms, frank in matter, it plainly intimated that we would have no favourable opinion of his religious and moral character if he did not honestly exert his powers on our behalf."

Such was Wilberforce's influence while he lived; but the effect of his actions on succeeding generations was an even clearer measure of his statesmanship. He set new tides flowing, which affected the climate of British public life for decades. We earlier quoted John Marlowe's strictures on the profligacy and venality of eighteenth-century public life and the "quality of heartlessness" which resulted. Marlowe goes on: "Men like Shaftesbury, and Wilberforce before him, set an enduring fashion in respectability which no politician could afford to neglect." Their influence remained, he added, "to soften the harsh light of Victorian governing class acquisitiveness and to tone down the consequent bitterness of antagonism between class and class, until much of that which they had hoped to achieve by compassion expressed in personal service was at length in some sort achieved by the democratic process which they had unwittingly encouraged."

Because Wilberforce's main challenge was to the rich and powerful, his contribution was specially important. As Shaftesbury and others donned his mantle they played a key part in the battle to bring more justice to the labouring masses, a battle which men like Keir Hardie, with the same Christian motivation, were to wage from the other end of society. It is doubtful whether the British labour movement would for so long have remained Christian rather than Marxist in its orientation without the impact of the Evangelicals on the governing classes.

In particular Wilberforce and his friends pioneered a new political integrity in an age of corruption and did much to transform the House of Commons from a club which cared for the interests of its Members into an assembly responsible for great issues of the commonweal. They also developed new ways of arousing public opinion and using it to influence Parliament. Lord Elton wrote of this influence: "Without roots in the nation a Parliament must wither; it can only survive and flourish if in constant and intimate contact with the electorate. . . . Intimate contact between the British Parliament and the British People dates from the Abolitionist campaign." It was the lack of such contact—and of the moral and spiritual content which "The Saints" sought to give to political life— which, Lord Elton believed, accounts for the failure of parliamentary institutions in some countries which established the form without first creating the spirit to enliven it. It was Wilberforce and his friends who ensured for Britain that "the new democracy would have its roots in religion."

Then there was Wilberforce's legacy to India and Africa. Coupland agrees with Furneaux that Wilberforce and his friends transformed British attitudes to these vast territories. "They planted in the public conscience of their countrymen," he wrote, "not merely a sensitiveness to wrong, but a positive sense of obligation towards these peoples. And in so far as the conduct of British Governments . . . was to be inspired throughout the coming century by the ideals of trusteeship, the honour of creating the tradition lay with them." Certainly the modern Commonwealth would be unthinkable without them, and even if we can now see that the British record of trusteeship was often marred by superiority or exploitation, the advance at the time was considerable.

G. M. Trevelyan, describing Abolition as "one of the turning events in the history of the world," emphasizes its amazing timing as far as Africa was concerned: "It was only just in time. If slavery had not been abolished before the great commercial exploitation of the tropics began, Africa would have been turned by the world's capitalists into a slave-farm so enormous that it must eventually have corrupted and destroyed Europe herself, as surely as the world-conquest under conditions of slavery destroyed the Roman Empire."

The timing was more than human. Wilberforce lived that higher statesmanship which consists in serving not his own interest but his God's. His obedience to what he believed to be the Will of God brought freedom to millions. Politics has been defined as "the art of the possible." Wilberforce, by his persistence, but above all by the spiritual element at the root of everything he did, again and again made possible in the future what had seemed impossible when he first tackled it. Such is the statesmanship needed in his and every age.

Epilogue

ONE OF THE COMMONEST illusions of our day is that the individual is helpless, unable to do anything to alter events around him. Seeing the allegedly powerful so often at a loss, the ordinary man concludes that external forces are too strong for him and lapses into the "helplessness syndrome."

This syndrome is particularly cruel because it drains the meaning out of life. Without vision the people perish, sunk in a slough of comfort, frustration or self-concern. Much of the mindless violence of our time stems from this sense that nothing constructive can be done.

The helplessness syndrome is at first sight a strange malady to affect mankind in the midst of a technological revolution which is said to make all things possible. One would expect people to be living in a fever of hope and opportunity. Surveys, however, show that fewer and fewer people think that the individual matters. Many of our most potentially creative people seem to think with the celebrated British painter Francis Bacon that "man now realises that he is an accident, a completely futile being" or with Kenneth Tynan who bewailed our "new and grievous plight, awaiting death in a universe without God, ungoverned by reason and devoid of purpose."

Christianity has always officially contradicted this view and proclaimed the infinite worth and potential of the individual. "I can do all things," wrote St. Paul, "through Him who strengthens me." But in reality the helplessness syndrome has deeply eroded such faith in many Christians. Many, perhaps a majority, feel with the Member of the House of Lords who replied to a recent survey, "the business of surviving and enjoying our leisure is all we are prepared to do." The more committed seem often to resort to one of two false alternatives: either to retreat into a ghetto of personal belief from which the affairs of the world are excluded or to adopt an almost entirely political stance which sees no need of conversion.

"Wilberforce," writes Pollock, "proved that a man can change his times, but that he cannot do it alone." He needed, in fact, a living God to change, remotivate, guide and strengthen him. He also needed a band of likeminded men and women to plan and work with him, and to help keep his aims and motives clear. Together they created the leadership which was required—and the nationwide groundswell which made that leadership effective.

Some will say that such things could happen in the Britain of the eighteenth and nineteenth centuries, but are impossible in twentieth-century societies. Organizations are so vast and forces so impersonal, they argue, that the individual can no longer initiate significant changes.

This, in my experience, is untrue. God is no less powerful today than formerly and men still have the capacity, if they will, to find his plan for themselves and events around them. Hundreds of people are initiating changes in conditions, large and small, all the time, and I personally have been privileged to see many such changes, some even on an international scale. The world today is waiting to see which countries will produce bands of committed people who will tackle together the seemingly insuperable problems of the coming age, as

Wilberforce and his friends tackled the deadlocked situations of their times.

Select Bibliography

Abey, C. J., and Overton, J. H. *The English Church of the Eighteenth Century.* Longmans, 1878.

Anstey, Robert T. *The Atlantic Slave Trade and British Abolition.* Macmillans, 1975.

Bradley, Ian. *The Call to Seriousness.* Jonathan Cape, 1976.

Bready, J. Wesley. *England Before and After Wesley.* Hodder & Stoughton, 1938.

Bryant, Sir Arthur. *The Age of Endurance.* Collins, 1942.

————*The Age of Elegance.* Collins, 1954.

Buxton, Travers. *William Wilberforce.* R.T.S., 1903.

Cecil, Lord David. *The Young Melbourne.* Constable, 1939.

Churchill, Sir W. *History of the English Speaking Peoples.* Cassell, 1956–8.

Colquhoun, John C. *Wilberforce, His Friends and Times.* Longmans Green, 1866.

Coupland, Sir Reginald. *Wilberforce.* Collins, 1923.

Edwardes, Michael. *The Necessary Hell; John and Henry Laurence and the Indian Empire.* Cassell, 1958.

Elton, Lord. *Imperial Commonwealth.* Collins, 1945.

Forster, E. M. *Marianne Thornton.* Edward Arnold, 1956.

Furneaux, Robin. *William Wilberforce.* Hamish Hamilton, 1974.

Greville, C. C. F. *The Greville Memoirs.* London, 1874.

Halévy, Elie. *A History of the English Speaking People in 1815.* Benn, 1949.
————*A History of the English Speaking People 1815-30.* Benn, 1949.
Hammond, J. L. and Barbara. *The Town Labourer.* London, 1917.
Hazlitt, William. *The Spirit of the Age.* London, 1825.
Howse, E. M. *Saints in Politics.* George Allen & Unwin, 1953.
Hyde, H. M. *The Strange Death of Lord Castlereagh.* Heinemann, 1959.
Jaeger, L. G. *Before Victoria.* Chatto & Windus, 1956.
Jones, M. G. *Hannah More.* Cambridge, 1952.
Kaye, Sir John. *Christianity in India; Administration of the East India Company.* 1853.
Knutsford, Baroness. *Life and Times of Zachary Macaulay.* Edward Arnold, 1900.
Lecky, W. E. H. *A History of England in the Eighteenth Century.* Longmans, 1918–25.
Marlowe, John. *The Puritan Tradition in English Life.* Cresset, 1957.
Morley, Lord. *Edmund Burke: a Historical Study.* Macmillan, 1867.
————*The Life of William Ewart Gladstone.* Macmillan, 1903.
Newsome, David. *The Parting of Friends.* John Murray, 1966.
Overton, J. H. *The Evangelical Revival in the Eighteenth Century.* Longmans, 1886.
Pasternak, Boris. *Fifty Poems.* Unwin Books, 1963.
Pollock, John. *William Wilberforce.* New York: St. Martin's Press, 1978.
Rattenbury, J. E. *Wesley's Legacy to the World.* Epworth, 1928.
Reynolds, Reginald. *The Wisdom of John Woolman.* FHSC, 1972.
Rosebery, Earl of. *Pitt.* Macmillan, 1891.
Rowsen, A. M. *Primates of the Four Georges.* John Murray, 1916.
Sherrard, O. A. *Freedom from Fear: The Slave and His Emancipation.* Bodley Head, 1959.
Stephen, Sir James. *Essays in Ecclesiastical Biography.* Longmans, 1849.
Trevelyan, G. M. *British History in the Nineteenth Century.* Longmans, 1922.
Trevelyan, Sir George. *The Life and Letters of Lord Macaulay.* Longmans, 1876.
Warner, Oliver. *Wilberforce.* Batsford, 1962.
Watson, Bishop R. *Anecdotes of Life.* London, 1818.
Wilberforce, John. *Private Papers of William Wilberforce.* T. Fisher Unwin, 1898.
Wilberforce, R. and S. *Life of Wilberforce.* John Murray, 1838.

————*The Correspondence of William Wilberforce.* John Murray, 1838.

Wilberforce, William. *A Practical View of the Prevailing Religious System of Professed Christians in the Higher and Middle Classes in this Country, Contrasted with Real Christianity.* London, 1797.

Williams, Eric. *Capitalism and Slavery.* André Deutsch, 1944.

Index